# $oft Money

# The True Power in
# Our Nation's Capital

# $oft Money

# The True Power in Our Nation's Capital

# A Novel

## By

## E. L. Burton

1stBooks - rev. 10/30/00

# Chapter - - 1

It had become a routine occurrence lately. Clay Danvers had begun the evening by trying far too hard to fall asleep, only to wake in a cold sweat hours before the annoying buzz of his alarm clock. Maybe it was getting to him, the reality of being a highly paid assassin. He had never fired a gun in his life because they scared him. By nature he was a pacifist, prone to settling his differences through his gift of communication rather than through violence.

This trend had begun early in his college days. For many in his generation, the 60's were a different time, a world that seemed so far away and different from today. It was during his sophomore year at Princeton that the Vietnam War had divided the United States and Clay was torn as to what to do. Which war to choose, the war at home against the establishment or the war abroad against the enemy? It was during this time and decision-making process that he met Tony. Tony was only a year older than Clay but in many ways seemed to be much wiser. He was tall, handsome, and articulate, with a smile that made you feel like everything was going to be all right. He had all the answers, and that is exactly what Clay was in search of.

Together, they fought the establishment and railed against the war effort. In the end there were no winners, only losers, both at home and abroad. The only thing that was accomplished was to divide a nation against itself and forever change the way we viewed our duty to our country and how we defended it, and ourselves.

He sat up in bed and shifted his body to the edge. Stabbing at the floor with his toes he tried to find his slippers, careful not to touch the cold wood floor. He made his way to the bathroom and rinsed his face with cold water. Staring at his reflection in the chrome fixture, he slowly rose to see a much clearer reflection of himself in the large mirror over the sink.

Clay Danvers did not like the person looking back at him. His hair had long abandoned him and what remained had begun the process of turning from its natural color to gray. Rather than

1

go the way of so many others by getting a hairpiece or plugs, he simply shaved it to mere stubble. He had toyed with the idea of shaving his head bald, but he couldn't bring himself to give up the little bit he had managed to keep.

As his gaze went from the top of his head to his face he could see that he was tired. The dark circles that surrounded his baby-blue eyes were an overwhelming example of it. His once powerful shoulders drooped, and his posture was poor. He looked more like a man of 70, rather than that of his true age of 56. Looking into the mirror at the overall spectacle of the man he saw versus the man others saw, he let out a bitter laugh.

Yes, he was an assassin. Yes, he did destroy lives, but his weapon of choice was not a gun or knife. It was a cleverly woven tapestry of words. He did not kill you outright. He just made you feel like you wished you were no longer among the living. Clay Danvers was, as he put it, a highly paid political strategist, or in terminology that was not so politically correct, a character assassin.

His function in life was to protect his employer at all costs and his current employer happened to reside at 1600 Pennsylvania Avenue, the home of the President, and also Clay's friend, Preston Anthony Wesley.

Startled back to reality by the phone, Clay left the gaunt face staring back at him in the mirror to answer it.

"Hello."

"Clay, it's Bart. We have a situation."

"What time?"

"5:00am."

As he placed the receiver back on it's perch, he realized just how short and how common these calls had become. There was no need for meaningless chatter, the calls were straight and to the point. Besides, in this town you never know who might be listening. He got up from the bed and walked towards the closet. Clay was somewhat of an eccentric. His manner was unconventional and his attire suited his personality. He rarely, if ever, wore a tie, and if he did, it was outdated by at least 20 years. He was most comfortable dressed only in jeans, boots, and a crisp dress shirt and sports coat.

2

As he readied himself for the events of the day, the ghosts of the disheveled souls and memories of the individuals he had helped to destroy drifted in and out of his thoughts. It was the bane of his existence, and lately it was the source of his sleepless nights. He knew that today was going to bring more of the same. He had made it so far by simply convincing himself that his role was a necessary evil, but at what cost? His reflection lasted only for a brief moment, and then he was out the door.

It was a twenty-minute drive to the office where the Group conducted its business. As Clay approached the parking garage, a security guard emerged and checked his identification. It was Old Sam. Sam was a funny character, kind of a real life version of Barney Fife. He took his job seriously, always looking at you like you were up to something.

"Mr. Danvers, nice to see you. A little early, isn't it?"

"Sam, early it is my friend. Early it is."

With that said, Sam pressed a button and the security arm smoothly swung up and the tire spikes retracted beneath the concrete floor. Clay patiently waited and then entered the parking garage. As he made his way off of the elevator, he saw that Bart Sullivan was impatiently waiting for him.

"So?" Clay said.

"What's our boy gone and gotten himself into today? An affair, or did someone find out he sold swampland to little old ladies? What is it this time?"

"Clay, you know as well as I do that skeletons always seem to find a way to fall out of the closet at the oddest times. You and I both know that when you are the President you have a 'kick me' sign permanently attached to your backside."

The President, like his predecessors, was currently under investigation by a special prosecutor assigned by the Justice Department. The original investigation was launched to probe his alleged affiliations with a suspected organized crime family. This stemmed from a law firm he was a partner in prior to his Senatorial run some 20 years ago.

At the time, he was cleared of any involvement in the case, but members of the opposing party were not about to let it die. The investigation was still pending. However, with his teeth

3

sharpened the Independent Counsel had begun to expand his investigation and was now chasing down anything that might bring the President down.

As Clay entered the conference room, he could see that everyone had arrived. He could never get comfortable with where they met. It was too formal and made him uneasy, but this meeting place was where the Group conducted all its business. It smelled of money, from the rich hardwood floors to the paintings that adorned the walls.

The conference table was one of a kind. In fact, it was a work of art, solid marble measuring fourteen feet long by six feet wide. It had been hand cut and polished to a brilliant shine by the caring hands of a talented craftsman. The chairs that surrounded the monolithic marble table were no less works of art, each one hand crafted with an artisan's blend of mahogany and leather. The room was an astounding mixture of elegance and technology, beauty and power.

Seated at the conference table was Mike Baker, President of Bytes Technology, the largest computer and Software Company in the world and the proud owner of these lavish surroundings. Seated next to him was Neil Reyna, founder and Chairman of the Board of Futurecare, the country's largest managed health care organization. Next was Patrick Cortina, the youngest of the Group. Patrick came into his fortunes the old fashioned way, he inherited it. He never worked a day in his life, but had all the connections that old money brings. And just sitting down was Bart Sullivan, President and CEO of GNN, the single largest media conglomerate in the free world. Seated in this room were four of the world's wealthiest men, each one with a vested interest in Preston A. Wesley.

"Gentlemen, now that we are all here, let's get started."

"Who wants to lay it out?" asked Clay.

Bart Sullivan stood and proceeded to activate a laptop computer, which was networked to monitors located in front of those in attendance. A single photo appeared on the monitors.

"Gentleman, as you know, we have several sources within the Justice Department.

Based on information received from one of those sources, we were able to obtain this photograph."

Seated on a park bench were the Independent Counsel Paul Justin and Lawrence Brazelton, a former attorney at Stoner, Winston & Kaplan.

"Bart, do we know the substance of this meeting?" asked Mike Baker.

"No!" came a short and stinging response, Bart continued.

"What we have gentlemen is history, a history that can be drudged up and brought back to life. We need to answer two questions right now. First, how much does he know? Second, what, if anything, does he plan to do with that information?"

Lawrence Brazelton was one of those sacrifices for the common good of the current administrations political machine. During the first presidential campaign he was loyal to the party line. In politics, loyalty is a commodity. Sometimes you owned it at no price, it was yours because you shared the same beliefs and philosophies. Other times it could be purchased. The currency was not always money, fear and intimidation worked as well. Most often it was a combination that included all the aforementioned ingredients.

Lawrence potentially had dirt on Preston A. Wesley, and it dated back to their time spent together as partners in the firm. There was a different truth behind the rise of Preston A. Wesley. For so long it had been kept guarded and safe from the prying eyes of the public and looked at with a blind eye by a media that was in love with Wesley. A truth so powerful even the men assembled had limited knowledge of its full scope.

Why now, and for what? That question had merit because there was always an angle. People never did anything unless they wanted or needed something. What did Lawrence want? As a body, the Group decided that contact would have to be made with Lawrence.

After a brief discussion, Clay Danvers was chosen as the most likely to make contact with Lawrence. It was Clay who had been the point man in the conversion of Lawrence Brazelton to the party line. He was a dealer in the commodity called loyalty. Their relationship went all the way back to their early days at Princeton prior to the entrance of Preston Wesley into his life.

It was there that they met and over the years their friendship had gone the way of many such relationships. It was divided by their ever-changing ideals, separated by the opposing forces of right and wrong, strained by the truth. The bond had been broken long ago. Too many things had happened since the idealistic days of their college lives and the life altering influence of Preston Wesley.

Clay wondered if Lawrence would welcome a sort of reconciliation and an extension of the olive branch. Or, would he see straight through him? Clay knew the latter to be the most likely, because too much had been taken away from Lawrence Brazelton, and the timing would be obvious. With the decision made, he knew that it would not be a pleasant reunion. Lawrence had something, something the Independent Counsel wanted. Clay knew that Wesley had some involvement with the Cordona family. Wesley had assured his keepers that his involvement was limited and that Lawrence represented the family.

The Group had assured Wesley that Lawrence would be spared as long as he played ball. Steps had been taken to insure that Lawrence got the message, and that is where it had ended. Or had it?

# Chapter - - 2

Lawrence Brazelton sat alone in his modest home in Falls Church Virginia. He had taken his finger out of the proverbial hole in the dike that represented his life. He had nothing left to give and no reason to live, but one. His loyalties had left him with nothing. From the outside he looked as though he had everything. His home and debts were all paid off. He was on the Board of a Fortune 500 company and earned a salary that most would envy. But he was empty.

Gone were the days of practicing law. His son had died during the Gulf War, and his wife had passed away from cancer shortly after that. He knew that he owed what he currently had to Preston Wesley. He also suspected he owed that same man for the loss of his practice, his son, and possibly even his wife. He knew how the commodity called loyalty was purchased. He had reaped the rewards as well as paid the price. Money and success by themselves mean nothing if you cannot share it with those you treasure most.

The reasons that Lawrence was alive today were somewhat confusing to him. He had narrowed it down to two reasons. The powers that be were satisfied that he posed no serious threat. The other reason revolved around the possible conscience of the man who had betrayed his trust and loyalty. Lawrence was betting on the first reason. Most men would have ended their life by now, but not him.

The information in his possession had kept his hope alive and given him a sense of purpose. His desire was that someday he would reclaim the life that used to be his. Contacting the Office of the Independent Counsel was the first step in that quest.

As the last ray of light filtered through the stained glass windows on the west side of Lawrence's living room, he realized that he had to reset the code on his Internet mail account. This mail account is where he stored the detailed information that could bring down the President. As he made his way into his den, he marveled at how far technology had come in such a short time. It had made so many things possible, and it was as safe as a bank vault for storing information.

Easy access by anyone to the World Wide Web made for an intriguing and interesting hiding place for his information, as well as the ultimate delivery tool. All the evidence needed to bring down a corrupt man was stored in a server somewhere on the World Wide Web.

In the event that Lawrence did not access his mail account every 24 hours and reset the send function, the information would automatically download and be sent to every news organization in the free world. Lawrence was not perceived as a threat due to the fact no one was aware of the information he possessed. He had not shown his hand until recently, but he had set into motion his plan to do the right thing and settle an old score.


Clay Danvers knew this was serious, he knew that Lawrence had the ability to damage his employer. How bad was not clear, but damage nonetheless. Damage that can take away points in the all important public opinion polls. That dictated how members of the Washington political machine made their decisions.

Long gone were the days when the rule of social and moral law determined the outcome of any decision made by politicians. Today a politician can do anything if they can garner favorable poll results. Hell, for that matter they don't even need favorable poll results if their cause falls in favor with the other political machine, the media at large. It shaped the public's opinion, through the lens of a camera and slick salesmanship.

No matter what side of the aisle you sat on, right or left, there was always someone there to tell you what to think and how to feel. Something had to be done, and Clay knew it. As the man in charge of spin control, another fancy moniker for assassin, he needed to know what Lawrence's intentions were. The only way to begin the discovery process was to make contact. Clay paused a moment before dialing, hoping Lawrence would take his call.

Lawrence was finishing his daily routine on the computer when the phone rang. He glanced at the caller ID box and noted the call was listed as anonymous, he hated to be bothered by tele-marketers and contemplated not answering the phone. He answered it anyway, feeling somewhat cocky and sarcastic.

"Hello?"

"Larry, Clay Danvers here, how the hell ya been buddy? Sorry it's been so long. When was the last time we talked ol' buddy?"

"Some fund raiser last fall Clay. To what do I owe the honor of speaking to the Boss's chief pit bull?"

"Ouch! I'm hurt Larry, I just thought we should get together sometime for a beer or something, talk about old times, laugh a little, maybe even talk about the future. What do ya say?"

"Anything specific Clay?"

"Hey, what's with the attitude? Can't a guy call an old friend and ask about getting together for a beer?"

Lawrence knew that a call from Clay Danvers meant bad news. He decided to remain cordial despite that fact.

"Sorry Clay, I didn't mean to snap. Things have been a little hectic lately. I would like that beer. What do you say about tomorrow? I have plenty of cold ones in the fridge, so stop by anytime in the afternoon. I am in meetings most of the morning, but I will be home after 3:00."

"Sounds good Larry, look forward to seeing you."

As Clay turned from the phone, he realized that the wheels had been set in motion. Lawrence Brazelton was not going to sneeze without it being recorded from 10 different angles in full audio and video. His life was now in a fishbowl on display for the members of the Group. He felt a twinge of guilt but quickly dismissed it.

Lawrence hated it when anyone called him Larry, especially that prick Danvers. But that was Clay, good at what he does and that meant keeping you constantly off guard.

Lawrence rocked back in his chair, folded his arms, and began to go over the conversation again, this time looking at the actual wording within the conversation.

As he reflected on the brief conversation, one phrase played over and over in his mind: "the future." Clay had to know about his meeting with Justin, but how? Why did he want to see him socially after so many years had passed? Why did he even care?

Lawrence had been careful. He had told no one of his meeting with Paul Justin, and Justin wanted the President so badly he would not jeopardize an opportunity by leaking information about the meeting. Had anyone seen them, or possibly overheard them? Wait, this is crazy. Nothing has even happened yet. I am losing it, thought Lawrence. Rather than feed the monster called paranoia, he decided to feed himself.

Clay turned to those in attendance and scheduled a meeting of the Group, as they were known, for the following evening at 7:00pm. They would discuss his meeting with Lawrence and decide on a course of action at that point. It was also decided that Lawrence was to be put under surveillance by members of a special unit under the guidance of Mike Baker. Everyone agreed and the meeting was adjourned.

As those in attendance filed out, Patrick turned to Clay who was still seated.

"Coming Clay?"

"Nah, you go on. Hit the lights before you go," Clay replied.

He sat alone in the dark conference room attempting to escape, if only for a moment. He realized that he was experiencing the same deep seeded anxiety that was responsible for his lack of sleep lately. Something was not right.

Maybe he was getting too old for this shit. Maybe it was time for him to hang it up and retire to the cabin he loved so much but never seemed to have the time to visit. He had promised himself that he would spend more time there. It was great therapy for him. Miles from any big city filled with too many people, just him his dog and his is fishing pole.

He reflected on how good it felt to just stand in the river with his waders on for hours on end. Time seemed to slow, space seemed to expand, and the sound of the running water and the wind through the trees put him in a trance. Catching fish was of little consequence. It was the relaxation he enjoyed. He swore he felt so relaxed he could actually hear and feel his heart beat and feel the blood flow through his veins.

Yes, he needed a change. He needed to feel alive again, to rid his body of this gnawing anxiety. Just a little longer, he thought. Just wait until after the next election. The President was finishing his second term, which meant that he could end his political career with the President, and finally retire.

Mike Baker picked up his satellite phone and dialed.

"You have an assignment: designated Watcher. Op specs will be posted as usual."

As the call disconnected, Mike knew that whatever Lawrence Brazelton did, whomever he came into contact with would be noted and cataloged. His home would be searched then wired, phone lines would be tapped, and even his garbage would be searched and tagged. Any sensitive information he had would be located. He knew you had to know what the other player's cards were before you bet the farm. Before any action was taken against Lawrence Brazelton, his hand would be common knowledge and his cards would be exposed to the Group.

The special unit he had just unleashed on Lawrence was a nasty bunch, no one knew of their existence other than the five members of the Group. The unit was known as the Dogwatch. Made up of five men with less than clean backgrounds, they were known by appearance only to Mike Baker and no one else. They had no background, no records and for all intents and purposes, did not exist.

They were the brainchild of Mike, and their primary function was to do clean up work for the Group. They were the tools by which many loyalties had been purchased and many skeletons disposed of. If a problem existed that Clay Danvers could not spin into favor for the President or for any member of the Group, the Dogwatch stepped in. It was their responsibility to simply make it go away, eliminate it.

It was a scenario that had played out many times. Often times it involved the simple art of blackmail. Other times the result was far more sinister and brutal, as was the case of a senior member of the President's cabinet. He found himself the possible target of a congressional oversight committee investigation.

This particular cabinet member knew a great deal in reference to several issues currently under investigation by the Independent Counsel regarding the President. The cabinet member had several strikes against him. The charges ranged from abuse of office to improprieties regarding gifts to an affair with a young intern. The possibility existed that the Independent Counsel could use this individual as a source of information against the President. The Group decided that rather than having this individual make a deal for immunity it would be in their best interest to silence him, permanently.

The matter was turned over to the Dogwatch for resolution, and that cabinet member died during what is being called, even today, one of the most brutal terrorist bombings of an American Embassy.

The spin by Danvers on this particular tragedy was also a masterpiece; One single shot of the President saluting as a tear traveled down his cheek while the coffin of that cabinet member was carried from the transport plane. An impassioned speech followed that promised the terrorists would be brought to judgment. The threat had been eliminated, and the spin was complete.

Mike called Clay Danvers. The call bounced from Clay's office to his cell phone. If Clay hadn't answered his cell phone it would have forwarded to his voice mail, and his pager would then alert him of the waiting message.

"Clay, Mike Baker. I forwarded your request and we are on track."

"Thanks Mike, appreciate the call."

Clay placed his cell phone on the passenger seat. He knew that the call was in reference to the Dogwatch. They had just been handed a bone, and its name was Lawrence Brazelton.

Clay began to wonder again if it was all worth it. He remembered a meeting he had had with the President shortly after one particular funeral. The President had looked him in the eye and quoted some obscure and often used reference,

" It is better that one man should perish than a nation should dwindle and perish in disbelief." At the time it had made sense, but how many men equal the President's version of "one" man?

Clay began to realize that he needed to bring the President up to speed on the situation, even though it did not add up to very much. He thought for a moment of trying to get back to that place in his mind. The river, fishing, the wind, he didn't have time for that. He had to go see the Boss and driving made reflecting difficult. He also wanted to look the President in the eye and ask him if he had told him everything about those days at the firm. He had to be sure if he was going to do his job. His job, he thought. He hated his job.

What had started as a promising career had turned into the nightmare that represented his life. He began to become agitated as the mental tug of war waged on in his head. He decided to call it a draw. He was tired, and he had a long morning ahead of him.

# Chapter - - 3

As Clay Danvers entered the Oval Office, President Preston A. Wesley stood to greet his friend, and with his hand extended they began to shake. After only a fraction of a second, the President tightened his grip and brought his left hand into the shake. If the President valued you, trusted you, then and only then did you receive the two handed shake.

This was the type of insight Clay had. Another sign of trust was when the President embraced you. These embraces occurred only after he shook your hand. The key was if he embraced you while still holding your hand, it was a sign that he did not trust you, that he wanted some space between you. If he let go of your hand and embraced you then that showed he had no reason to keep anything between you.

He had learned these idiosyncrasies from years of watching his friend in action.

"Clay, what a pleasure it is to see you. Please sit. Can I offer you something to drink?"

"No thank you, Mr. President."

Clay thought how funny it was to know a man as well as he knew Preston Wesley, and for some strange reason he could not call him by his first name. He had not called the President by his first name since the day he was inaugurated. Not during interviews for television, radio or print, even when it was just the two of them. Maybe it was out of respect for the office, or maybe it was simply just a subconscious reaction. He didn't know, and frankly, he didn't care. He had other more pressing issues to fill his time and mind with.

"So Clay, to what do I owe the pleasure of your visit today?"

"Well Mr. President, we may have a problem."

"Before we go any farther, I need to know something, and I hate to even have to ask."

He paused trying to form the question that he knew would sound accusatory no matter how he phrased it. Clay being who he was, decided to follow a piece of advice his daddy had counseled him with and that was to shit or get off the pot.

"Sir, have you told me everything I need to know regarding your time at the firm? More to the point Sir, is there any connection between you and the Cordona family other than what you have told me? The purpose of this question deals directly with my visit here today. I am not going to beat around the bush. We have a photograph of a meeting that took place yesterday between Paul Justin and Lawrence Brazelton."

The President's expression did not change but the tone of his one word response was mixed with surprise and confusion.

"Lawrence?"

"Yes Mr. President," replied Clay.

The President rose from his chair, turned, and faced the window, hands behind his back, neck slightly drawn down and held tight. Even though Clay could not see if his eyes were open or if they were closed, he knew by the President's posture the answer to his question.

Preston Wesley had always been an ambitious individual. During his life he had always naturally gravitated toward being a leader. People seemed to always want to be around him, even as a child. He had a way with words and was blessed with the capacity to maintain the flow of a conversation. As a member of his high school's debate team, he soon learned he had the ability to win practically any argument. It was at that time he decided to go into law.

It was during his college experience he met his wife, Saundra. They were both running for President of the sophomore class. As good as Preston thought he was, she was better, and she defeated him in the election. He remembered hating her for beating him. Losing to a woman, to him that was the ultimate defeat.

That hatred didn't last long at all, for even as it had begun, it soon ended. She was bright, attractive, and so very charming. They flirted, flirted with dating, and Preston soon realized that if he was going to go places, he needed her. What a team they would make. To say they married out of love might be a stretch. It was more out of admiration and the pursuit of a common goal. Who knows he thought, maybe that's what love truly is.

After college they both went to law school and graduated at the top of their class. Knowing that his future was in the public arena of politics, she wanted to begin their grassroots march to the Capital at ground zero. Even though Preston Wesley didn't necessarily believe that he could be President, Saundra did. Sure he had the ambition and he did have the dream, but Saundra saw the reality. Rather than work for a top firm, they went to work for a modest firm in Atlanta, Stoner: Winston & Kaplan.

The President turned from his prolonged stare out the window and began to relate to Clay events in his life that had brought them to the present situation.

"Clay, when I was seventeen I had the chance to meet the President of the United States of America. Our high school debate team had won National Honors, and as a reward, we had the privilege of visiting the White House. Just as you shook my hand today, I shook hands with the President, right out there. At that moment, I knew that this was where I wanted to be. The way people looked at him and treated him, the way he made me feel. I wanted that. When I got home, I began to formulate a plan. Can you imagine that? I was a seventeen-year-old kid writing an action plan to get to the White House."

The president reached down to pick up a pen from his desk. At first, he simply looked at it, possibly remembering the physical act of writing his action plan. Slowly, he began to twirl the pen between his fingertips.

"What I failed to understand at seventeen were the realities of how you got here. My intentions at the time were so noble, and I had no way of knowing the little pieces of me that I would have to sacrifice, the compromises I would have to make along the way. You know the drill, you do this for me, and I will do that for you, even if what they asked was somewhat less than honest. You just rationalized it away in your mind, telling yourself that the ends truly justify the means by which you reached your goal."

"Because in your mind, your goals are honorable and good, your visions clear. You realize you could not make them a reality until you got to the top. Then and only then could you right the wrongs and make the world a better place."

The President paused to collect his thoughts and then continued.

"So, here we are. Rather than go back and correct the wrongs and unbend those compromises, we are still trying to hide them. We bury them, treat them like a nuisance and act like we are the victims."

Clay knew the President was a good man. He also knew that he had made some dangerous alliances during his political career. Those alliances were not about to see their President throw it all away in a momentary attack of conscience. This had been the topic of many discussions within the Group.

The President was troubled by some of the compromises and tactics that brought him to the White House. Clay knew that both parties were aware of the conditions that came with their support. He also knew that the President had not disclosed everything to the men who had made him. And that had created a problem. Like his daddy used to tell him, it don't make much sense to fix the barn door after the horses done run off. Had he disclosed the truth in the beginning, they could have eliminated the threat before it had materialized.

"Yes Mr. President. Please go on Sir."

"The firm did work for the Cordonas. Most organized crime families need legitimate ventures to run money through. You know the drill."

There was a long pause. A look of pain and anguish washed over the face of Preston Wesley.

"I was the one who did the work for the family. I told you that it was Lawrence, but it was me. The other members of the Group know as well, however, the extent of my involvement has remained my secret, a secret shared by Lawrence and myself. I asked for the resolution of the problem to be left to me, and the others agreed."

The pain in the President's face began to take on a genuine tone and texture. Clay watched and listened as the President continued.

"He went along with it only because I had found out that he had had an affair, a rather unconventional affair for a heterosexual married man. Rather than have the affair exposed to his family as well as his colleagues, he agreed to maintain that they were his clients. The men who were committed to my rise agreed, and it has remained a topic that has never reared it ugly head since."

"Lawrence knew where I was headed, and he knew that we would have to spin this into our favor. He knew that the voting public could not tolerate a presidential candidate who was tied into the Mafia. He agreed to change the billing records to reflect billable hours as his. All the documentation that reflected my involvement with the Cordona family was destroyed. The time sheets, memos all destroyed. And with that done, he agreed to be the sacrifice, the one to lose."

He paused a moment before continuing, Clay was held almost catatonic. The shock of what he was hearing was slowly seeping its way into his consciousness.

"I promised Lawrence Brazelton that he would be taken care of. I felt I owed him that. He has since endured the loss of his practice, his son, his lovely wife, and on top of all that, a world-class character assassination. If I had told you everything, you and the others would have had him terminated then and there. You wanted it all? Well, there it is. Now what are we going to do to remedy our current situation?"

Clay was shaking off the effects of the initial disbelief and managed a laugh inside. "Our" situation, when it was bad, it was always "our" situation. The Group had already begun the process to determine what the ultimate resolution would be. The only thing the President needed to hear was that everything was under control, which is exactly what Clay told him.

The President knew each member of the Group. They had contributed substantially to all his campaigns. Campaign finance laws regarding soft money contributions had made it possible for them to funnel millions of dollars towards their candidate. They held numerous fundraisers for the party, they were the elite, and they were the ones who had real power in the Capital.

They were silent partners whose hands were in the pockets of many of the old guard, as well as the new. This group ran

Washington and dictated much of the policy. Not even Clay Danvers knew the full extent and reach of the Group.

In many ways the Group had played Clay, just as the President had played him, telling him only what they thought he needed to know. What was unique about this was that Clay Danvers was the only person who knew of the existence of the Group as a whole. He believed it was because this was the first time the Group had actually manipulated someone into the White House, and they needed someone who had the President's ear, someone who drew far less attention than they would.

Individually, they had all reaped the rewards of having a "friend" in high places. Bart Sullivan had seen several communications-friendly bills signed. Additionally, he had some help in gaining contracts within China.

Neil Reyna had assisted the President in drafting the Healthcare Reform Act. This increased the long-term viability and profitability of Managed Care Organizations nation wide. With that growth came profits, and with those profits came mergers, and with those mergers, an HMO giant was born, Futurecare.

Mike Baker owned the largest Software Company in the world, which was under investigation by the Justice Department. The investigation was in reference to allegations of intimidation and unfair competition within the computer industry. Many people viewed Bytes Technologies as the last major monopoly of the 90's. His problems were reduced to a slap on the wrist and some petty fines.

This was the type of power money can buy. The Group was into the President. He knew it, but what he didn't know was the lengths at which the Group would go to keep that type of influence in check. The President did know of the Group's existence and of its true motives and tactics. Over the years he had convinced himself otherwise. The Group had a vested interest in keeping the current party in control of the White House. As was customary, the Vice President was almost a lock for the party nomination.

The Group was not done yet. They still craved the two things that have historically plagued men, power and money.

They were not going to let this administration suffer a blow so close to the next election. Rather than promote an agenda that would benefit this nation as well as the world at large, by addressing such issues as Health, Energy, Agriculture and the Environment. Instead, they pursued an agenda that would guarantee the propagation of their own power and fortunes. It would be done at any cost and with no regard to people or the degradation of the environment.

# Chapter - - 4

In a dark abandoned warehouse in an industrial park that would look no different in any city in the country, sat Conner Braxton. As he turned from the phone, he clicked the icon on his computer desktop that connected him to the Internet. He made his way around the web to a rather inconspicuous looking Web Page. He began downloading the updated version of the Web Page to his laptop. The broadband satellite Internet connection eased the process.

He watched the blue transfer indicator fly from left to right and listened for the computer-generated voice to say those magic words, Files Done. He terminated his Internet connection, accessed the newly downloaded version of the Web Page, and ran it through an encryption program. Mike Baker had provided the encryption software, and it was way ahead of anything currently possessed by Uncle Sam.

There is in excess of 350 million sites on the World Wide Web. If someone had found this obscure web site, they wouldn't even know what they were looking at. The recent technological advances in computers had provided a new form of communication for today's criminals. The file was done running through the encryption program, and Conner Braxton was now reviewing his next assignment.

Clay Danvers found himself back in his home, alone again. Well, not completely alone. He had his dog, Springer. Springer had been a good friend and companion for Clay. She never judged him, never expected anything other than to be fed and walked. And that dog loved to go for walks. Every time she heard the word "walk", she went nuts. He decided that was what he needed as well, a walk. He turned to Springer and said;

"Wanna go for a walk?"

The dog went wild. She jumped in the air and then ran around in circles. It brought a much-needed smile to his face. As they walked down the street, Springer was in her hunting mode, back and forth in front of Clay. Smelling everything and tugging on the leash the entire way.

In his mind, Clay began to float back to that cabin in the mountains. He needed a break, and he needed some time away from the rat race that was his life. When they returned, Springer made a beeline for her water bowl, and Clay made a beeline for his. He opened the refrigerator door and took out a cold beer. Before opening it, he rolled it across his forehead. He opened the freezer and pulled out frozen lasagna, and popped it in the microwave.

After he ate, he retired to his bedroom and turned on the television. He had a habit of turning on the TV and not watching it. Sure he looked at it, and if you saw him you would swear he was watching it, but he wasn't. He just liked the noise, the distraction. It made him feel less alone. It was not long before he was asleep.

*"WHAT!"*

Clay sat straight up in bed, looking around the room as if he were expecting to find someone, he was breathing heavy and not quite sure where he was. As his mind caught up to him, he realized that he was alone, except for the TV and Springer staring at him from the foot of the bed. He looked at the clock.

"Quarter to four," he muttered.

"I gotta get a life."

He turned off the television and sat in the dark. He knew what was troubling him. Deep down inside himself, in a place where no one likes to look, in a place where you hide your pain, your choices, and the consequences of those choices, he knew. Some people could live their entire life and never go there, but for some strange reason he was spending more time there lately. It was as if a cold hand reached out and grabbed him, frozen by the grip and not able to see the face beneath the black shroud, it made him sit and watch his life, frame-by-frame, choice-by-choice. Never saying anything, just making him watch.

He realized that he did not like what he was watching. He knew he had to do something, but the owner of the cold hand had not imparted the solution. It had just informed him of the problem. But what was the solution, and why was this all happening now?  He just sat and thought.  Springer startled him when she jumped off the bed and headed out the door.  He glanced at the clock and noted that it was 5:45am.  He was stunned and surprised at the amount of time that had passed.  He would have to rush to make his 7:00 interview scheduled for that morning.

Conner had finished reviewing the assignment the Dogwatch had received the night before.  He had posted a notice on a computer bulletin board that read, "Snoopy come home."

The other four members checked the board every morning and would know by that message to be here by 7:00 am.  Conner looked at his watch, it was 6:59am.

The first to arrive was Jason, followed by Carlos, Victor, and finally Nathan.  These men were as anonymous to each other as they were to the public at large.  No need for last names and conversations of life outside their activities, or any social interaction.  It was business.  It paid well, and it paid to know as little about your partners as necessary.

"Good to see you all could make it.  I realize that this may be a little early for you girls, on account of your beauty sleep and all."

The team muttered and gestured towards Conner.

"We're on," Conner said.

"I have prepared a dossier on our current target.  This assignment has been designated, Watcher."

"For now, our objective is to become very familiar with our target.  We are to have no contact with him.  He cannot know of our presence or of our intentions.  We are simply taking the role of his shadow for now."

Conner paused briefly to glance at the assembled men to see if they were paying attention or if there were any questions.

"This is strictly an intelligence gathering operation.  Our employer wants to know everything there is to know about this man, what he eats, who he talks to, where he shops, banks, and has his laundry done."

A hand is raised.

"Yes Carlos?"

"What exactly are we looking for?"

Conner smiled and replied.

"Information."

That brought a puzzled look from the team.

"Our employer has asked that we obtain any information in this man's possession that even hints at the name Preston A. Wesley. **Any** and **All** information."

"You mean the President?" replied Carlos.

"Yes, that's right, the man himself."

The only person that knew the identity of their employer was Conner. Conner never asked questions and did not know if that's where the chain of command began or ended. He didn't care and neither did the other members of the team. The only thing they cared about was the money and the fact that their employer had cleaned their dirty pasts and returned them to society to do the things they were best at, as well as enjoyed.

They never questioned their assignments. They knew that they could be erased from society at any time.

"We know what to do, so let's get to it."


Lawrence was at that stage in his morning routine that bothered him most. He had dressed and was standing in his closet staring at his ties. His wife had always picked out his tie in the morning. He never seemed to pick out the right one. She had often commented that he was color-blind or suffered from fashion illiteracy. Remembering those comments brought a smile to his face. He grabbed a tie and began to tie it as he walked. He stopped briefly at the mirror in the foyer to check his knot. With a half smile, he thought to himself that she would have hated this tie with that suit.

Lawrence checked his watch. It was almost 9:00am and he was running late. As he pulled out of his driveway, he noticed a truck from one of the local cable companies, and said to himself in a low almost unrecognizable tone of voice.

"Cable must be out again, now I know why I switched to the mini dish."

He didn't even give it a second thought as he drove off.

When the car rounded the corner at the end of the street, the team flew into action. A van from the gas company pulled into the driveway on the side of Lawrence's house. Shielded from the street traffic, the four remaining members of the Dogwatch exited and began to make their way into the house. Bypassing the house alarm was easy. Most home security systems are just for show and could not keep a true professional from gaining access.

Each member of the team had an assignment. The point man, Conner, was perched at the top of the utility pole on the outside posing as the cable man. Jason was the computer expert, and he began by first attempting to access Lawrence's computer.

After several attempts, he had still not gotten in. This indicated to him that there were probably passwords protecting his files. Rather than attempting to break the password, he simply attached a keyboard bug. At a glance, the connection did not look out of place. It was fitted with a microchip, which recorded all of the keystrokes. The keystrokes would be recorded, then transmitted back to the command center. Once they were received, they would be run through a computer filter to determine exactly what had been entered.

Carlos was responsible for the placement of all the video monitoring equipment. He installed pinhole cameras throughout the house. The cameras were roughly the size of a dime, and they measured 25mm high X 25mm wide X 10mm deep. Equipped with an electronic shutter to compensate for changing light, they provided 1024 lines of resolution for a sharper picture. They required a hole of only a 1/16" in diameter for viewing and were easily concealed anywhere.

Victor worked placing standard UHF room transmitters in strategic locations, as well as outlet transmitters, which were placed in appliance outlets. For recording all incoming phone traffic, both spoken as well as data, he utilized line-powered taps installed in each phone outlet. These were located behind the phone jack itself on the line and were not detectable due to the frequency at which they operated.

Nathan was given the unenviable task of doing a physical search. He knew it was a nowhere assignment. What idiot would leave his cards exposed for all the other players to see? He searched anyway, with the thought that sometimes the best hiding place is in plain sight to comfort him. All Nathan could think about past this moment was that it was his duty to be the garbologist of the mission. Garbology is fast becoming a common tool for criminals.

A person's trash can provide a tremendous amount of information. It can tell you what they eat, whom they have talked to, where they have been, and even how often they have sex.

Wiring Lawrence's house took less than 20 minutes. As the gas truck backed out of the driveway, Conner was making his way down the utility pole. It was all in place. Lawrence Brazelton's life was now a fishbowl in the private showroom of the Group. Conner packed up his gear and began his trek back to the warehouse.

# Chapter - - 5

Clay arrived at the local affiliate of GNN for his scheduled interview. Slade Wright, the man who would be conducting the interview, met him in the reception area.

"Good to see you Clay. I trust you didn't have to wait long."

"Not long at all Slade."

"Hope you're ready. I am not going to go easy on you this time. The word is the Independent Counsel is not going away. He has a lot of support from the Presidents opposition. It is a well known fact the President has problems."

"The way your talking sounds like I will be the next Oliver North. Only I don't have chest full of medals," replied Clay.

Clay had to chuckle. He knew the benefits of having the man who owned the largest media empire in the free world on his team. He knew that the questions would come at him more like softballs rather than Major League fastballs. What made him laugh was that most journalists prefer you to think they are in control and out to seek the truth. Reality is, the truth is what the boss tells you it is, and according to Bart Sullivan if you looked up truth in the dictionary, you would see a picture of Preston A. Wesley.

"Here we are. Let makeup work on that ugly mug and I will see you on the set."

"It won't take long, I am already stunning," replied Clay.

Just as he had expected, the interview was a breeze. The President came out the hero, and the Independent Counsel was the epitome of evil, out to destroy a good man who had done such wonderful things for the people, the economy and the children of this fine nation.

Slade Wright was just another pawn in the game of spin control. He followed the party line, as well as the agenda of his employer. Clay knew that as long as he could keep the Independent Counsel on the defensive, he would have the time to mount an offense.

As Clay reveled in his momentary victory of the day, his reality began to surround him. He began to realize what was causing his sleepless nights and his tremendous anxiety.

"I am tired of taking care of everyone's shit, of cleaning up everyone's mess. I am starting to feel like a damn janitor!" his voice sounded loud in the car.

And a janitor is exactly how he felt. He was always being called out to clean up the mess anytime, anywhere.

As the team rendezvoused at the warehouse, they began to set up shop and go on live at the Brazelton location. All of the surveillance could be done from the warehouse. The majority of the equipment utilized satellite and microwave technology. They had even found a way to track Lawrence using his cellular telephone, which allowed them to know his location at all times without having to tail him too closely and risk exposure. Acquiring his ESN, or his Electronic Serial Number did this.

Using the signal that identifies a cellular phone, Lawrence could be tracked as long as his phone remained on. This is done through a process called TRAC, Threshold Range Algorithm Code. With the old analog phones, it basically sent out a signal searching for cell sites to accommodate its use.

With the new digital technology, the opposite occurs. The cell sites send out a signal to your ESN to ensure line quality and maximum signal strength. By monitoring his ESN and utilizing a computer map overlay, a two-man team could follow his every move by triangulating his position using the cell sites. Since Lawrence carried his phone everywhere, it was ideal for following him even on foot.

"We are online gentleman, locked, cocked and ready to rock."

"Excellent Jason. Now lets have a look."

As Conner looked at the monitors that displayed practically every angle and elevation of the Brazelton home, he smiled.

"If this guy farts, we will know," he said.

It was just before 3:00 as Clay pulled into Lawrence's driveway. He knew he was early and hoped Lawrence was home. He also knew that whatever happened here today would be on the record, therefore he had to be careful. He rang the bell and waited. He turned to leave figuring he was too early. At the same time, Lawrence pulled up and parked next to his car.

"Clay, you're early. Is that good or bad?"

Clay smiled and extended his hand.

"It's all good, and it's good to see you."

As Lawrence began to shake his hand, he felt a small piece of paper between their hands. Clay grabbed Lawrence and began to hug him like good friends do. He whispered in his ear.

"Act normal, invite me in, and excuse yourself to the bathroom."

As they broke their hug, Lawrence invited him in. As they entered the front door, Lawrence deactivated his alarm.

"Clay, you know where the kitchen is. Go grab us a couple of cold ones. I will be right with you. I need to go, if you get my meaning."

"Sure thing Larry."


As the Dogwatch team members waited in the warehouse for the first sign of life, the silence was broken.

"Sir, we have action!" shouted Jason.

Conner hurried over towards the monitors. As he watched, he saw Lawrence enter through the front door and deactivate his security system. Another man followed him. Conner knew the man as a contact of Mike Baker, and he recognized him from several television programs.

Lawrence made his way down the hall to the bathroom. He shut the door and opened the note. It simply read:

**"They Know"**

Lawrence sat on the floor, put his forehead on his knees, and began to feel a wave of panic wash over him. The blood rushed from his head, and he began to feel dizzy.

"What have I done?" he whispered to himself.

"Ok, they know, but they don't know everything. They can't. All they could possibly know is that I met with Justin."

He knew that they would not make a move until they knew what his motive was and more important what his information was. He knew that his house and his life were an open book by now, and he would have to be cautious. Clay's visit was more than likely a feeling out process, used to gauge his demeanor and establish any possible motive. But Lawrence was confused. Why would Clay hand him the note? Why let him know? Slowly the dizziness passed, and Lawrence made it to his feet. He looked into the mirror as he contemplated the question.

Clay stood in front of an open refrigerator staring at several different brands of imported beer. He knew he owed Lawrence something and felt like he had done the right thing. He was being loyal to his employer and at the same time he had given the heads up to his friend. A friend he had long abandoned.

If the Group wanted Lawrence they would have to do their own dirty work. Strangely, Clay felt a wave of calm run through him. Maybe this is what was lacking in his life, a certain sense of balance and fair play. He didn't like what had happened to Lawrence, especially now that the President had told him everything.

Lawrence finished staring at his reflection, realizing that the answer was not going to be found looking at himself in the mirror. He flushed the toilet, ran the water, and washed his face. Walking down the hall and through the dining room to the kitchen, he found Clay standing in front of the refrigerator.

"So, what's your poison Larry?"

"Just hand me whatever Clay."

They both twisted the tops off their beers simultaneously and took a long hard drink. This was an awkward moment for both of them because they had no idea where to begin and each man had no idea what each other's motives were. It was like a dance. Only neither one was leading. Clay broke the silence by speaking first.

"Larry, I know things have been rough on you over the years. God only knows you have been through a lot with Laura and Charles."

Laura was Lawrence's wife, who had died of cancer, and Charles was their only child and he died during the Gulf War. Charles death came during the early days of the Wesley run for the White House. Lawrence had always blamed himself for the

32

death of Charles. He believed it was a message meant to keep him in line. It was investigated, and in the end, it was classified as a case of friendly fire.

"I am not going to tell you I know how you feel, because I don't. I just want you to know you have a lot of friends who care about you, and none of us want to see you go and do something stupid."

"What makes you think I am feeling bad, and more important what would give you the idea that I was going to possibly do something stupid Clay?"

"This may be a big town with a lot of people my friend, but you gotta know that nothing stays a secret for long," replied Clay.

"Unless they have you and your kind to follow them around with a shovel and a flashlight to keep it all covered up nice and neat," Lawrence bit back.

"Look Lawrence, I don't want to fight. I just want you to be careful."

"Clay?"

He was cut short as both men turned, and in walked Kelly. She was a hair under six-foot tall, brown hair with brown eyes, and a smile like no other. Kelly had been seeing Lawrence for quite awhile. She met Lawrence shortly after the death of his wife and had been a blessing to him. Many times Lawrence had contemplated ending it all, but it was Kelly who kept him going. She put things in perspective for him. She understood his pain and helped him in ways no one else could.

Lawrence cared for her deeply, and what he was doing now was for her. He knew as long as certain individuals remained in control, anyone he loved was in jeopardy. He didn't want anything to happen to Kelly. He refused to watch another life cut short because he lacked the character to do the right thing.

As Kelly entered, Lawrence noticed that her eyes met with Clay Danvers and a puzzled look seemed to come over both of them simultaneously. That was odd Lawrence thought. As far as he could remember, the two of them had never met, and he did not think that anyone even knew he was in a relationship. It caused him only a momentary pause.

"Hey honey. I hope I am not interrupting anything," she said.

"No, not at all. Clay just dropped by to catch up on old times. I wasn't expecting to see you until tonight."

"I know, but I called your office, and they said that you had finished for the day, and I thought that I would surprise you."

"Where are my manners? Clay, this is Kelly Ford."

"Pleasure to make your acquaintance Ms. Ford."

"Likewise Clay, but I didn't catch your last name."

"Danvers, " Clay replied.

"I thought I recognized you. I have seen you on several news programs."

"Just doing my part, and don't believe everything you see on TV."

"That is the best advice I have ever heard come out of your mouth Clay," said Lawrence.

"Now be nice Larry," replied Clay.


While the small talk continued, Conner and the other members of the team were fixed on the monitors back at the warehouse.

"How is the audio Victor?"

"Five by five Sir."

"Video?"

"Crystal Sir."

"Jason, good work with the relays. Looks like we are receiving both ends beautifully."

"Thank you Sir. Long-range surveillance is wonderful, isn't it Sir?" replied Jason.

"Ok gentleman. Jason, Nathan and I will remain here. Victor and Carlos, I want you on the road ready to move with the target if and when he leaves. We will stay in touch via the SAT phones. No landlines gentleman. Now let's move people."


Clay thanked Lawrence for the beer and the company. He told Kelly it was a pleasure to meet her and excused himself. As Clay approached his car he turned to look at the house of Lawrence Brazelton and thought, good luck old friend.

Clay got into his car and backed out of the driveway and drove off.  He struggled with the urge to look in the rearview mirror to try and catch one last look at Lawrence.  He tried to remember the point in time when their friendship had begun to fall apart.  He began to feel responsible and the guilt only increased as he continued down the road.

# Chapter - - 6

Kelly walked over to Lawrence and took him into her arms. He melted into her embrace. She always made him feel safe, and for a brief moment he did feel safe. Kelly had come into his life in a moment of complete and utter despair. She took his hand and led him from the darkness that had been his life after the death of his wife. Out of nowhere she appeared.

Lawrence thought to himself that when a man rescues a woman, they refer to a knight in shinning armor riding in to save the damsel in distress. But what is the reference point of when a woman rescues a man? The mental picture of Kelly riding in full battle regalia wielding a sword and coming to his aid made him smile. They broke from their embrace.

"Do you know what you mean to me Kelly?"

"No, why don't you tell me."

"I am being serious Kelly. Do you know?"

"I think so, and you mean a lot to me."

He wanted so badly to say those three simple words, the words that are spoken every day by people. They were words that for some are genuine and for others just a means to an end. In his case those feelings were genuine, and maybe someday he would be able to say I love you.

He knew she was aware of his feelings, and he knew that she was prepared to exercise patience and wait for his healing to be complete. That is why he had to make the slate clean. He knew she deserved it, and he wanted some form of a life again.

"Thank you Kelly, for everything."

"Peanut, is everything alright? You seem so far away from me."

Kelly didn't necessarily like the name Lawrence, and she knew he hated it when anyone called him Larry, so she called him Peanut. She had come up with Peanut one night when he was standing in front of a mirror looking at his reflection, and his body shape reminded her of the Peanut man in the TV commercials. He didn't mind. As a matter of fact, he thought it was cute. So, the Peanut man was born.

"Just one of those days. Just one of those days."

"How about I cook you a nice dinner, and we pop a movie in and spoon in bed?" she asked.

"No, I need to run to the office and pick up some paperwork that I forgot. Then I was thinking about taking my favorite lady out for a nice quiet dinner."

Lawrence knew that his house was probably bugged and the last place he wanted to be was there. He had known that this time would come. He couldn't run the risk of exposing anything or letting them know he knew he was being watched. Then it hit him, maybe the visit by Clay was meant to scare him, to make him panic and show his hand.

Now was the time to be cautious. He had to watch every move and not risk his objective, which was to expose Preston A. Wesley for the man he truly was. First stop was the office. He had to reset his mail account, and he did not feel safe in his house anymore.

Lawrence picked up his keys and his cell phone, placing it in the breast pocket of his suit. He mused that when it came to cell phones, men competed to see who had the smallest, unlike the typical arguments over size.

As he exited his house, he walked to the mailbox and along the way casually looked around for anything that appeared to be out of the ordinary. Children were getting off a school bus on the corner, and his neighbor was retrieving the mail. By all accounts everything looked normal.

He thought to himself that winter seemed to come earlier every year. As the sun retreated the temperature seemed to plummet. He closed the mailbox as Kelly motioned for him to hurry because she was getting cold.

Lawrence made his way towards his office, and he noticed that traffic seemed to be light for this time of day. He soon realized that while he was trying to get to his office, everyone else was doing the exact opposite. He glanced over at Kelly as she stared out the window, and he could see that she was deep in thought. He reached over and gently touched the back of her hand, tracing over each finger, eventually intertwining his fingers with hers. Kelly interrupted her deep thought for a moment to smile at him and squeeze his fingers, as if to comfort him and let him know everything was all right.

The beauty and peace of the moment was interrupted by Lawrence's cell phone. As he released his hold on Kelly, she turned and continued to stare out the window. Lawrence reached in his pocket, pulled out his phone and answered.

"Hello?"

He paused.

"Hello?"

As he closed the flip on his phone he said.

"Must have been a wrong number."

Lawrence was unaware of the car following him and the fact that the call was no wrong number.

Victor looked at the digital readout on the screen of his laptop and turned to Carlos.

"Works every time."

Referring to the fact that they had just intercepted Lawrence's ESN and could now track him. Victor then called into base to let Conner know that the target had been located and they were locked on.

Lawrence didn't bother to go through the hassle of parking in the parking garage. Instead he parked in the front of the office building and let Kelly know he would only be a moment. As Lawrence entered his office, he activated his computer and as the system was booting up, he shut the blinds. He accessed the Internet and then accessed his mail account.

The process was relatively easy because he had designed it that way, in and out. He also had the foresight to establish a mail account that could be accessed from any computer with a modem. The only mail he ever received was the occasional piece of junk mail. He never opened them. He just simply deleted them. As long as the account was accessed and the outgoing mail's send time changed, the information remained in what he referred to as a state of suspended animation. He shut the system down and left his office.

As he got off the elevator and approached the front door, he realized that his original excuse for coming to the office was for paperwork. He realized his hands were empty, so he turned and hurried to catch the elevator door. When he got back into his office, he grabbed a manila folder on his desk without even looking at its contents, turned, and exited once again.

As he walked through the front door of the office, Kelly waved, and he picked up his pace a bit. He was hungry, and he felt better now. He had bought himself some time to figure out exactly what his position was. This was indeed much like a chess match, and each opponent would have to take his time during and between each move.

The green Chevrolet Blazer pulled away from the curb at about the same time as Lawrence had pulled away from his office. The tail car was at a comfortable distance, far enough away not to reveal their presence, but close enough to move if needed. Carlos turned to Victor and broke the long-standing silence.

"Remind me to talk with Conner about wiring the car. I guarantee we are missing out on valuable intel."

"No praw bro," replied Victor.

"What did you say? Speak English you fool. You sound like an idiot."

"Whatever, that's the way they are talking on the street. You gotta keep up with the times my man."

"I am not your man you moron. Just drive the damn car, and keep your dumb ass jive talkin to yourself."

"No praw," he said.

Carlos ignored his partner's continued efforts at reshaping the English language. His first instinct was to simply bitch slap him back to reality, but those feelings passed and it was back to the business at hand. He returned his focus to the present assignment and tuned out the meaningless banter of his partner.

Lawrence turned towards Kelly to ask her what she felt like eating. He found himself looking at her, admiring her for the way she carried herself. She was physically attractive, as well as intellectually stimulating.  Like most women, she was a mystery, hard to figure out at times and somewhat reluctant in discussing her past life.  He had left it alone, figuring that if he pried too much it might scare her off.

"So, what do you feel like?"

"Italian!" she said.

"Funny, you don't look Italian to me."

He reached over and began poking her on the arm.

"And you don't feel Italian either."

"Nice to see you haven't lost that sense of humor Peanut."

"Italian it is.  How does the Risotto Café sound?" he said.

"Fantastic.  I love their clam sauce."

"Risotto's and clam sauce it is," he said.


Conner excused himself and retreated to a make shift office in the corner of the warehouse.  There he booted up his laptop and preceded to update the Web Page that would be viewed by Mike Baker and run though the encryption process to reveal the progress report he was expecting.  His employer expected to be kept in the loop at all times and in every aspect of the Dogwatch progress and operation.

As he ran his fingers rapidly across the keyboard, he informed Mike of the team's progress.  Lawrence's house had been wired, and he was under constant surveillance.  The operation was in its infancy and naturally there was no news of capturing any crucial information.  That would have been too easy and too much to expect in such a short time.

This report was merely a formality, a way of letting his employer know that the Dogwatch was gnawing on the bone and would get to the meat of the matter in due time.  He knew that Mike was one for detail after all he was a businessman and approached everything by cutting to the chase and getting to the bottom line.  Conner liked it that way because he knew that his reports could contain substance in a condensed form, rather that fluff contained in a mass of meaningless banter.

So he continued touching on the salient points of the surveillance, as well as his standard guarantee that the team would deliver.  As he finished, he could not help but smile as he closed the Web Page. The necessary updates, when deciphered, would reveal the intended message.

Mike sat alone in an office located directly behind the conference room, which the Group used to conduct its business. The office was what could be considered a geek's ultimate dream. He was preparing his brief, as well as anticipating the Groups meeting later that evening. His satellite phone began to chirp and he reached towards his belt for it.

"Yes?" he said.

"You have a message," Conner replied.

And with that said, he placed the phone back on his belt clip. As he accessed the Web Page he used to communicate with the Dogwatch, he marveled at how proud he was for initiating this form of communication.

Web Pages numbered into the millions worldwide, and they were expanding exponentially day by day. When Mike felt the need, which was often due to his extreme paranoia, he simply created a new page. It might be something substantial that provided valuable information and links to other sites. Or it might be just another homepage showcasing mom, the kids, and the family dog, with a bio and a reference to what the family did for summer vacation. To anyone else it would be meaningless. However, if you had the key, you might be amazed at the information that was contained therein.

As the encryption program finished, his field report flashed on the screen. It was as expected, nothing earth shattering, just an acknowledgement that the game had begun, and the dog had the scent. The hunt was on.

Clay did not bother to go home after his meeting with Lawrence. He was dealing with too many emotions. He knew that he had a meeting to attend that evening, one which he was not looking forward to. He had called his neighbor and asked if she would go over and feed Springer, explaining that he was going to have a late evening. She understood, like the many times before. She enjoyed taking her son along for the chore, claiming that it had saved them the expense of buying a dog of their own.

Clay needed the time to think. He was at a crossroads in his life. It felt like he had bought a ticket on a one-way train when he became involved with the Group. It was a train that had no stops and no way to disembark gracefully.

He knew in his heart of hearts that the Group would interpret any attempt at leaving as a threat. And he knew what ultimately happened to anything or anyone that posed a threat to the Group and their agenda. He would become a casualty brushed aside by the Group and he would pay the ultimate price, his life for their peace of mind. He knew he had to do something, something to make his life right. He needed to feel good again.

When he handed Lawrence the note that had made him feel good. However small the gesture was, he knew he had done something to help a good man in a bad situation. For a brief moment, Clay thought that he could fight the system from the inside, but soon came to the realization that that was impossible. You can't fight City Hall, and you damn sure couldn't fight the Group.

Clay had an hour before the scheduled meeting so he pulled into a park, found a quiet place, and parked. As he laid his head back on the headrest, he began to think. He just needed to rest a moment. He was so tired. For a brief moment, he was able to ease his inner turmoil, but unfortunately, it did not last.

The anxiety that had plagued him for so long, deprived him of sleep, and robbed him of any happiness began to slowly build. It felt as though it began in his heart and radiated outward enveloping his entire body and filling the car. He needed to escape, to elude these feelings that followed him like his shadow.

An almost peaceful calm and serene look began to emerge from his troubled wrinkled face. His cheeks began to flush and he began to see through clear eyes. If he listened carefully enough, he swore he could hear a voice. The voice was saying come home. At that moment, Clay reached under his seat and removed the 9mm Smith & Wesson his father had given him prior to his death.

Without a moment's hesitation, he quickly chambered a round, placed it in his mouth, and fired. Clay Danvers was free, and the train had one less passenger. The last thought of Clay Danvers life was the hope that Lawrence would understand the meaning of his special delivery.

# Chapter - -7

Mike Baker was annoyed. You could tell that by the irritated look painted on his face. You could also see his annoyance beginning to turn into anger.

"Did we agree on 7:00? I seem to recall that we agreed on 7:00. Could someone please tell me why it is now 7:30, and we have no idea where our Mr. Danvers is?"

"Mike, calm down. I am sure there is a logical explanation. Clay has never been late before," replied Bart Sullivan.

"Well, has anyone tried to call him?" asked Mike.

"Yes, and we haven't been able to reach him," said Neil Reyna.

"Doesn't that strike anyone as a little odd? I mean he is always available," said Mike.

Mike was growing more and more impatient as the seconds ticked by. The room was silent, and he began to pace and mumble to himself. He could not tolerate incompetence, and in his view, being late was a classic sign of incompetence. The silence was broken by the sound of the elevator reaching the top floor.

"It is about time," replied Mike to the sound of the doors opening.

That relief soon turned to further frustration, as it was only Old Sam who exited the elevator.

"Mr. Baker, Sir. I am so sorry for the interruption. I know that I am not allowed to disturb you, let alone come up here, but I think you should know that I overheard a broadcast on my police scanner," he paused.

"Out with it Sam. We don't have all day here," Mike said.

"Well Mr. Baker, I think Mr. Danvers may be dead," said Sam.

"What? What are you telling me, and be specific," Mike said.

"Yes Sir. A call came through reporting the discovery of a body in a parked car at the park just north of here. The description of the dead guy and the car sounded pretty much like Mr. Danvers."

"Is that all?" said Mike.

"Yes Mr. Baker. That's all, and that's when I rushed on up here. I knew you were expecting Mr. Danvers, and I know he is never late for one of you all's meetings, so you know I figured, well."

"You are rambling Sam," Mike said.

"Yes Sir," replied Sam.

"Thanks Sam. That will be all. See that we are not disturbed, under any circumstances. Now go," and Mike waved him off.

Mike turned momentarily to the Group as if to say something, only to turn to the window that overlooked the city. With his arms crossed behind his back, he began to twist the ring on his finger and appeared to be deep in thought. Mike Baker was a man who was always in control. With that control came the feeling of invincibility and an ability to always get his way.

Make no mistake, nobody ever gave him anything, what he had, he had earned. His methods were considered by some to be unorthodox, even underhanded. However, to those in the business community, he was respected, a man with vision. That vision was in a state of temporary blindness at the moment. His control seemed to be slipping. With the recent events surrounding the Lawrence Brazelton situation, coupled with the news he had just received, he was feeling far from invincible. His mind was racing, but he had to act fast.

Mike knew that the Group looked to him as a sort of unofficial leader. Although the Group was made up of equal parts with each member having equal control, he was regarded as the unspoken leader. Maybe it had to do with the fact he was the richest man in the world. He had to laugh at that thought. He could feel the eyes of the other members on him. The silence in the room was eerie, and he realized he would have to speak.

Mario escorted both Lawrence and Kelly to a quiet table in the rear of the restaurant. He pulled the chair back, removed the napkin from Kelly's plate, and gently placed it in her lap. As he assisted her in moving her chair forward, he said:

"It's a been too long since your last a visit. I was a starting to feel like you no like a Mario no more."

"Mario, we love you. We save this place for special times," replied Lawrence.

"I tell a you what, no menus tonight. You let a Mario prepare something a special."

"Thank you Mario. You are the best, and please, you pick the wine as well," Kelly said.

"For you it would be a my pleasure," and with that, Mario was off, waving his hands and shouting directions as if he was directing a Broadway play.

"What is with you Peanut? I mean I have not seen you this happy in, well, I am not sure," said Kelly.

"Good company, good food. What can I say?"

"Well, you can excuse me for a moment for starters. I need to go to the ladies room."

As she walked off, Lawrence asked himself the same question he had been asking for some time now, why me? What does a woman like that see in a man like me? Looking down at his stomach as it extended well past his belt, he shook his head and smiled. It was then that he noticed that he had brought in the folder he had retrieved from his office earlier.

Curiosity got the best of him and he opened it, it was his mail. He had several small eccentricities and having a neat and organized desktop was one of them. He could not tolerate people who were disorganized. His secretary was kind enough to accommodate this particular quirk and placed all his mail inside a folder prior to setting it on his desk. As he looked through his mail, he discovered that it was all pretty much the standard fare. Except for one large plain envelope. It had no return address and no writing of any kind, just a sticky note that read:

*"This arrived by courier just after you left."*

Odd he thought. He opened it and it contained a single 8 X 10 photo of the President playing golf with three other men. Not strange in and of itself. Every President played golf because it was a great photo op. He recognized two of the men, Mike Baker and Neil Reyna, and the third looked familiar. Yes, it was Bart Sullivan, the media mogul.

The three men in the picture with the President represented monetarily the equivalent of most countries gross national product. He turned the photo over, and there was a note scribbled on the back,

*"You can change the Golden Rule."*

He knew what the golden rule was. He who had all the gold makes the rules. But what, if anything, did that have to do with the men in the picture. He noticed something else. There was a small red "X" on a corner of the restroom in the background of the picture. What the hell did this mean? Just then Kelly approached the table and he hurried to put the contents of the folder together quickly, stuffing it under his leg on the seat.

"Miss me Peanut?" she said.

"Uh, yea," he replied.

"Oh no, I must have the wrong table. You are a completely different man from the one I was with. The man I was with had a smile on his face and a carefree happy attitude. Maybe you can help me find him? I know I left him somewhere around here."

"No, I am fine. It's me, see," he said with a smile on his face.

"Ok, that's better. I thought I lost you. So what were you looking at?" she said.

"Oh it was nothing. I picked up the wrong file. Turns out it is just my mail from today," Lawrence replied.

"Do we need to swing back by the office later?" she asked.

"No, work can wait. Let's enjoy dinner, and I am warming to your idea of spooning in bed later," he said.


Mike slowly turned from his position in the front of the window. As he looked at each individual in the room, he began to speak.

"Well, it looks like we can get started," he said coldly.

"Bart, get someone out to the park and see if we can establish the identity of the man they discovered. If it is

Danvers, I will get our people to his house. We can't have anything that links him to us.

Mike turned again to face the window and continued to speak.

"If this is true, we have a major problem. This is all that Paul Justin needs to fuel his little private war against the President. We need to step up our efforts in the Brazelton affair. Lawrence is a wild card. If he has anything, now is the time to know."

"Mike, if it is Clay, why?" asked Patrick.

"Who knows, and who cares. Remember, ours is not to question why," Mike replied.

Bart turned to the Group as he returned the telephone receiver to its cradle.

"I have a news team headed to the park. They have instructions to contact me immediately with any information."

"Very good Bart. Now if you will excuse me, I need to place a call," Mike said as he made his way to the door.

As the news van arrived at the park it was already blocked off and being handled like a crime scene. An officer stopped the van and indicated that there was no press allowed at this point, and a statement was forthcoming. Brenda Castillo, was an aggressive up and comer at the local affiliate of GNN. She directed the driver who doubled as her cameraman to park the van. She pulled the visor down, adjusted her hair and checked her makeup. She then told her driver to wait in the van.

She was instructed to verify the identity of the victim, and that was it. No news just information. She wasn't sure why, she just knew the message came directly from the boss. She exited the van and adjusted the mini skirt she was wearing. She was a master at reading people, and she knew everyone wanted to talk. Their mouths may utter the words "no comment", but their eyes and body language told a different tale.

"So, who's it going to be?" She said to herself as she surveyed the mass of people, some rushing and others just standing around.

"Bingo," she said.

Standing at a corner of the taped off scene was an officer who seemed a little too happy to be there, a rookie perhaps, or maybe just a guy who was having an exceptional day. He definitely looked like a talker. She was a clever interviewer, and she never went for the throat with the first question. She would watch you for a moment, try to pick up any personality characteristics, which she would then key on and use to lure you in. She could make you feel like a friend, and she would have made a top-notch saleswoman. But news was her passion.

While she watched, she noticed him remove a pack of cigarettes from his front pocket. She moved towards him like a cat, undoing two buttons on her blouse as she walked.

"Got a light?" she asked.

The officer swung around and was greeted by two very well-positioned breasts. With his eyes fixated on her chest, he answered.

"Yes Ms. I do," he said.

"Oh, a real gentleman, thanks," she said as he reached out and lit her cigarette.

"I don't want to sound rude, but I can't comment on the situation ma'am." he said.

"Please, call me Brenda, and I wouldn't want to get you in any trouble," she said.

The next few moments were filled with a pained silence. It was all part of Brenda's methods, and it appeared to be working. The officer began to look back and forth and she could tell he was just aching to talk. She knew that it was in most people's nature to talk. People craved attention. It was a form of acceptance. The key was to make someone feel that they have something you want, and sometimes the most effective way is to simply act as if you don't care. It then becomes necessary for the person to share their knowledge to prove that you should care. She could tell he was aching to prove it.

"I know you, don't I? I mean I have seen you before, on TV?"

"Gorgeous and perceptive" she replied. Let the floodgates open she thought.

"Listen, this is off the record. I mean this could cost me big," he said.

"I don't want much. Just tell me who the stiff is."

"The car is registered to a Clay Danvers, and we are pretty sure it's him. Strange thing is, we were instructed to shut the scene down and wait for the Feds to arrive. That's all I know. He must be some important guy. When the Feds arrive, all we will be doing is crowd control."

"Listen, you have been a big help, and I won't say a word. It's not a story until it's a story, know what I mean?" she said.

She smiled, winked, turned, and walked away. She had what she wanted. Mr. Sullivan had just asked for confirmation on the identity of the man. Brenda didn't ask questions, especially when it was the boss. She had career ambitions. She wanted to make it to the network, and favors for the boss could ease the climb to the top.

Each member of the Group was off in their own world, talking on their cell phones, accessing information on their computers. Bart Sullivan walked into the room, and it was reminiscent of the old EF Hutton commercials. All eyes went towards him, and all ears waited for him to speak.

"It's confirmed, Clay is dead."

"Murder? Suicide? What are we talking about here?" asked Patrick.

"We don't know at this point, and that is the least of our immediate concerns. We have to be sure that there is nothing that ties Clay to this group. His death is already going to draw too much attention as it is," Bart said.

"At this point I am going to pull two of the men we have working Brazelton to clean Clay's house, as well as that damned cabin of his," Mike said.

"Bart, check with your sources. We need to know who is handling the investigation. I also want minimal news coverage regarding this. We need some time."

"Mike?"

"Yes Mr. Sullivan."

"The Feds are handling the investigation.  My source at the scene confirmed it with the locals.

"Mike?"

"Yes Patrick."

"Aren't you worried about cutting the surveillance on Brazelton?"

"Don't worry yourself.  We still have one card to play, one more person on the inside," said Mike.

"We need to be back here by 11:00pm.  This is going to be a long one.  Everyone knows what to do, so let's get to it."

# Chapter - - 8

Lawrence deactivated the alarm system, and still he couldn't help but feel uneasy about being in his own home. It was an odd feeling, to know that you were being watched, and at the same time having to act natural. The funny thing about acting natural is that it is all subconscious and spontaneous. How do you act natural when that is all you can think about? His head was spinning as he pondered that thought.

"I am going to take a shower, I'll see you in bed," he said.

"Would you like some company?" was the quick reply.

"No, I'll only be a minute, go ahead and get comfortable, I'll be right out."

"You're no fun! Where is your sense of excitement and adventure?" she said.

"Hunting is an adventure, amusement park rides are exciting, I don't think personal hygiene qualifies," he responded.

"Alright, alright, you win, I'll be waiting," she said.

She casually walked towards the bedroom undoing her blouse. As she reached the bed, she kicked off her high heels and laid her blouse on the footstool. Then she unzipped her skirt and let it fall to the floor. Her relationship with Lawrence was not merely sexual. The relationship was based more on friendship. She felt lucky to have finally met a man who was not interested in simply having sex.

With Lawrence she had a friend, a companion, someone who would listen when she needed to talk and someone who could just hold her when she didn't feel like talking. So why did she feel so bad? Why was she filled with such anxiety? She didn't need to ask herself those questions because she already knew the answers. She thought only for a moment that if she acted like she didn't know, maybe the truth wouldn't hurt so much.

Funny thing about the truth she thought, people always say the truth can set you free. But what they don't talk about is the fact that it can make you a prisoner.

Nathan turned his attention briefly to Conner and commented.

"Man, now I know why I love this job so much!"

Conner made his way over to the video monitors and observed Kelly lying on the bed completely naked. She appeared to be deep in thought, with a blank fixed stare.

"This isn't a peep show Nathan. If you want to get a thrill, do it on your own time," he said.

"But I am," he replied.

"Just keep it real, and stay focused. Got it!"

With that, he turned to walk away, but not before catching one last glimpse and smiling as he returned to his work. After only a few seconds, he felt his phone vibrate on his belt. Conner was a private man who didn't like to share his business with anyone. Not to mention the fact that he hated the high pitched ring of the little portable phone. He shut the door to his office to gain some privacy.

"Yes?"

It was Mike Baker.

"Conner, we have a situation. It appears as though Mr. Danvers is no longer among the living. I need a cleanup crew at his house yesterday," he said.

"I understand. Consider the house cleaned."

"Conner, no lose ends, and be DQ about it. The Feds have the ball, and we need to be in and out, got it?" Mike said.

Conner knew that Mike meant damn quick and quiet.

"Yes Sir," he said.

Conner hit the end button and opened the door to his office. Nathan, who was now joined by Jason, turned and watched as Conner approached. Both men were now enjoying the show that was being played out on the monitors.

"If you two aren't too busy, I have a job for you. Besides, I thought I told you to be a perv on your own time."

After a moments pause, he shouted at both men.

"Just get you asses over here."

"Yes Sir!" was the response in stereo.

"I need you two Romeos to double time it over to this address. You're on cleaning detail. No loose ends, and I want

54

you to make it look like a model home, like no one lived there. You may not have a lot of time, a lot of bureaucratic red tape on this one. That should give you a window. Any questions? Good, now get on it."

Conner sat alone in the warehouse. He could not help but feel uneasy about having the team chasing two different angles. He thought to himself, this is how mistakes are made. The only thing that brought him any comfort was that Lawrence had no idea what was happening.

He walked over to the bank of monitors and took up where the others had left off. Watching Kelly on the bed was the closest he had been to a woman in some time.

Kelly was now under the covers in bed and almost asleep. Lawrence was a little more modest when it came to nighttime apparel. He wore only his boxer shorts to bed and was proud of it. Even though Kelly referred to him as the Peanut man, for a man his age, he felt like he looked pretty damn good.

"Umm, you feel so warm, and you always smell so good after you shower. Do you feel better?" she said.

"Being with you always makes me feel better."

"You are so sweet. What did I ever do to deserve you?"

"Funny you should ask that question. I have been asking myself that exact same thing since the first time we spent any time together," he said.

"You're an easy man to love Lawrence Brazelton."

"I don't think I have ever heard you say that you loved me. Is this a watershed moment? Are we expanding our relationship and moving on to the next level?" he said.

"I'm tired, can we just lie here and enjoy each other?"

"Something I said? I thought we were on a roll," he said.

"Just hold me Peanut, just hold me."

He cuddled up to her back, and they assumed their favorite position, the spoon. He was confused about what had just happened. Did she love him? Did the words just slip out? And why did she just freeze up when he pursued it? He liked to hear those words. It had been so long since he shared those words, those feelings with anyone. He didn't think that it would ever be possible to love again. But there he was, staring love right in the eye.

He pulled her even closer to him. He placed one hand on her breast and cupped his hand over her nipple. He loved her nipples, and he loved the length and the feeling he got, as they grew hard. He kissed the back of her head and closed his eyes.

It was late, and Mike hadn't left the office. He sat and patiently awaited the arrival of the other members of the Group. He had handled his end. The Dogwatch was now sanitizing Clay's home as well as keeping tabs on Lawrence. The future of the Group had been dealt a serious blow.

They no longer had a point man for liaisons with the White House. Clay Danvers was a unique link and one that was going to be difficult to replace, if not impossible. No member of the Group could take his place, because that would be an open invitation to trouble. Each one had garnished some sort of favor or gain from their relationship with the President. Clay's position as a life long friend and well-known strategist had made him a perfect asset for the Group.

That asset was now gone, gone for good. The question at hand was what were they going to do about it? First things first, damage control was the primary objective. Bart Sullivan entered the conference room.

"Mike, it has publicly been made official. The man has been identified as Clay Danvers. He was the victim of an apparent suicide. It is currently being treated as a homicide until the autopsy and ballistics tests can be run. The Feds, due to the identity of the victim, are running the investigation. The President has been informed and has scheduled a press conference for 8:00am, at which point he is going to thank Clay for his loyal friendship, as well as his service to this nation. He will declare his intentions of not letting the matter rest until it is resolved. He will ask that the memory of his fallen friend not be remembered in vain."

"Do we have anyone in the White House or in the Bureau that we can trust?" asked Mike.

"Some low level agents, but other than that, no one that I am aware of," replied Bart.

With that said, the remainder of the Group had arrived and assembled in the conference room. The SAT phone on Mike's belt began to vibrate, and he excused himself. He retreated to his office, which overlooked the conference room.

"Talk to me," he said.

"Sir, the Danvers location has been cleaned. Our boys made it out just as the suits arrived. We retrieved Mr. Danvers computer, as well as all his files. The boys were careful, no one will ever know we were there." Conner said.

"Very good, and Mr. Brazelton?" Mike said.

"Sleeping at the moment," Conner replied.

"Very well, keep Mr. Brazelton under a microscope. Things are going to heat up with the events of the evening unfolding. I want what he has, and then I want him dead. Do you read me?" Mike exclaimed.

"I read you, loud and clear," replied Conner.

And with that, the conversation ended and Mike returned to the conference room.


Lawrence had not moved at all. He remained entwined with Kelly despite the fact that he couldn't fall asleep. He was wide-awake. With so many things running through his mind, the visit by Clay, the package he had retrieved from his office, his involvement with the Independent Counsel, and his feelings for Kelly. It seemed as though everything was moving much too fast. He paused for a moment and gently squeezed Kelly as she slept so peacefully in his arms. He could feel her heart beat and it helped calm his own heart.

He gently slipped from around Kelly and rolled out of bed. He stood over her for a moment and noted how beautiful she looked as she lay in bed. He gently pulled the covers over her naked body.

He retreated to the kitchen wearing only his boxer shorts and drank a cool glass of water before going into his home office. He sat at his desk and was shocked at how cold the leather on his chair felt against his bare legs and back. He turned on his computer, and as it warmed up, he took out the photo that had been delivered anonymously to his office earlier that day. He knew that he was probably being watched, so he was careful to keep the photo directly in front of him, close to his chest.

The computer chirped at him and he entered the password that would allow him access, "payback." As the computer continued its startup process, he again turned his attention to the photo.

"What am I looking at?" he mumbled.

He turned the photo over and read the phrase again.

"You can change the Golden Rule."

He turned the photo back again and stared at the figures on the photo, again noticing the small red X on the corner of the small building in the background.

"I guess I am going golfing, but where?"

Turning his attention to his computer, he accessed his Internet account and began a search for the AP wire service. Once on the AP page he narrowed his search by accessing the AP photo gallery. Again narrowing his search by specifying only photos of President Wesley playing golf. That brought him 195 entries.

"I see he hasn't lost his love for the links," he thought.

Lawrence went from photo to photo in search of the one that matched the one he had in front of him. Two hours later as he viewed the last of the 195 photographs on the wire services page, he was amazed. There was no match. He closed out the Web Page and leaned back staring at the ceiling. He was unaware of the camera looking down at him from the smoke detector.

He was frustrated and tired. He contemplated accessing his mail account and resetting his password, but decided that he would do that at the office due to his paranoia.

He turned off his computer, tucked the photo into the Wall Street Journal, and put it into his briefcase. He made his way back to the bedroom and took a moment to watch Kelly as she slept. She looked so peaceful he thought. He slipped under the covers and cuddled up against her.

Jason Wheeler sat in the operation center for the Dogwatch. He had left Nathan behind to watch the Feds and finish up. As he snacked on powdered donuts and drank coffee, he watched the recorded video feed as Lawrence went about his business. When Lawrence returned to bed, Jason rose and walked to a small room that consisted of two small cots that the team members used to catch a quick nap when time permitted. Jason did not have to speak, Conner was already aware of his presence.

"What?" Conner said.

"Sir, the subject was active earlier," he replied.

With that said, Conner rose, wiped his eyes, and proceeded to follow Jason to the bank of monitors. Jason queued up the tape of Lawrence in his study, and both men watched.

"Sir, we can gain access to his computer now. The chip in the keyboard bug shows his password as *payback*. Furthermore, he instituted a search of the AP wire services photo gallery specifying any pictures of President Wesley playing golf."

"Interesting, wait, back the tape up," Conner said.

"There, what is that he is looking at?" Conner asked.

"I am not sure Sir. He kept it out of the view of the camera. However, he did tuck it in a newspaper and place it in his briefcase after he was done surfing the net," Jason replied.

"Very well. When he leaves for the day, I want you to access his system remotely and download any information that he has on it," Conner said.

"What did you and Nathan do with the items you removed from the Danvers house?"

"In the other room Sir, even his garbage," Jason said.

"We didn't find anything that was out of the ordinary. I can tell you that his dog is no guard dog," Jason said.

"If it is not too much of a problem, maybe you and your partner can sort through it and condense your findings and give me the Readers Digest version for the boss," Conner said.

"Consider it done Sir," replied Jason.

Conner returned to his cot and made another attempt at sleep. As he lay there, he began to go over his options on retrieving the item that Lawrence had been so careful with and had placed in the newspaper prior to putting it into his briefcase.

He knew it had to be significant. Therefore he had to know what it was.

# Chapter - - 9

Preston A. Wesley sat in the Oval office with his chair facing the window. He was deep in thought and you could tell that he was troubled, troubled by the events surrounding the death of his friend. He had just met with him and could not believe that it had come to this. They had been so close for so long, shared both success and failure, but at what cost?

He wanted answers. How and why could something like this happen? He had to fuel his personal outrage. He had to justify his deep sense of loss and remorse. To not do so would make him inhuman. Unfortunately for him that is just what he was becoming. He knew the how and the why. He witnessed first hand the pain and anguish that Clay had gone through. What separated them was that Clay did not let the madness continue.

The world of politics was twisted. What was good was now perceived as evil, and what was evil, was now viewed as acceptable. Clay had escaped. To most people he may have taken the cowards road. To Preston Wesley, Clay had taken the only road available. The only coward was Preston Wesley.

He knew that he would continue to feed the machine that had created men like him and results like the death of his friend. He would continue to rationalize the events of the day and gloss over the truth to serve a purpose, his purpose, and his agenda. When you are the President, it is about your agenda, your legacy. The intercom interrupted his train of thought.

"Mr. President, everyone is here," said his executive assistant Karen Bowers.

"Very well Mrs. Bowers. Show them in."

The focus for the meeting would be the death of Clay Danvers and the attendees were Chase Walters, the President's Chief of Staff, James Montgomery, the President's Press Secretary, Stephanie Glenn, Attorney General, and Kenneth Jeffreye, Director of the Federal Bureau of Investigations.

"I would like to thank you all for being here. This is a difficult time for us. Those of us who knew Mr. Danvers well, know of what I am speaking," the President said.

"The reason I have called this meeting is to make sure we are following proper protocol. Director Jeffreye, I have asked that the Bureau conduct the investigation. Mrs. Glenn, do we have a problem with jurisdiction?" the President asked.

"No Sir, since we are treating this as a possible homicide, and since Mr. Danvers was employed as a consultant by the current administration, we are looking at a possible federal crime," she replied.

"Good. Mr. Montgomery, I want a press conference scheduled for early afternoon. I had hoped for a morning press conference but I felt it necessary to have this meeting prior to any statement. Please make it brief and sincere. Include our thanks for Mr. Danvers many years of loyal service, as well as my deep sense of personal loss. You know the drill," the President said.

"Yes Sir. Would you like any comments as to the status of the investigation?" he asked.

"Only that it is currently under investigation, and we will release more details as they become available."

"Consider it done Sir," he said.

"Mr. Walters, I want every accommodation made to the office of Independent Counsel regarding this matter. I don't want him to have any excuse or any reason to try and tie this tragedy to this office. Make it known that he is to have access to any individual as well as any material pertaining to Mr. Danvers involvement with this office."

"Yes Sir," replied Chase.

"If there are no other questions, that will be all," the President said.

When the President asks if there are any questions, he is really saying that the meeting is over. As they all rose to go about their assignments, the President motioned for Chase Walters to stay. The President went to his desk, opened the top right hand drawer, and deactivated the recording devices within the office.

"Mr. Walters, I need for you to make certain that any sensitive information contained in Mr. Danvers office be removed. I would also ask that you keep me personally informed of whom the Independent Counsel asks to speak with regarding this matter. Furthermore, please see that Mr. Danvers home is paid a visit, as well as his cabin. I am sure that his home has been visited. However I am confident that his cabin has not been."

"Yes Mr. President, and I will keep you informed as information is acquired," he replied.

"Very well. That will be all," the President said.

With the meeting concluded and his office once again to himself, the President sat down at his desk and turned once again to face the window.

Lawrence woke to the familiar smell of coffee and what he thought might be eggs of some sort. He rolled out of bed, stretched, and walked to the kitchen. He found Kelly standing at the counter holding the morning paper and she had a troubled look on her face.

"Good morning little miss sunshine," he said.

There was no response.

"Hello, is anyone home?"

She looked up at him with a stunned look on her face.

"I'm sorry. Have you seen the morning paper?" she said as she handed it to him.

"Of course not, you know I just got up," he replied as he took the paper from her.

He looked at the front page and was stunned. The headline read:

*"Death visits the White House"*

And just below the shocking headline it read:

*"Close friend and political confidant of the President dies in what is being called a possible suicide."*

Lawrence went numb as he looked at the picture of Clay Danvers on the front page. He could not move. He wasn't sure whether he was even breathing. After what seemed like an eternity he turned to look at Kelly. Her mouth was moving but he couldn't hear anything. That's odd he thought, he focused on her mouth and it was moving in slow motion, where was the sound?

Mike Baker spent a sleepless night in his office. He was not prone to panic. He had faced his fair share of adversity in his life, and he had battled through each and every situation, proclaiming victory in the end. He would know victory again. He just wasn't sure exactly how and when he would win this particular battle. His mind was working on a new point of contact, a new inside man. He looked down at the list he had been working on. One name stood out, Chase Walters.

Chase had come to the White House via Mike Baker. Prior to his entry into the political arena, he had been a very successful consultant, one that Mike had used on a regular basis on several mergers and acquisitions. Their relationship was purely professional, and Mike was not sure exactly how he would enlist the services of Mr. Walters. He did know he had the potential to kill two birds with one stone, first by continuing to have the President's ear and second, by having an inside track to the next administration.

Mike knew that if the Vice President was successful in the next election there was a strong possibility that he would retain the services of Chase Walters as his Chief of Staff. Yes, Walters was the man. The only question was, would he play ball, and would he play for Mike's team?

First things first, Mike knew he had to get the approval of the Group prior to the recruitment of Walters. Each member of the Group carried a very special PDA. It was the brainchild of Mike, and he believed that someday everyone would carry such a device. It would be used for communication, information storage, as a form of electronic payment for goods and services, but for now the Group used it primarily for communications and information sharing. It was small, about the size of a checkbook. It contained a writing area that utilized a graffiti style, handwriting recognition program.

Once he had finished composing the message informing the Group of a meeting later that day, he simply hit send. In an instant the message was digitized and sent out over the air and simultaneously each was informed of the meeting and his intentions to reveal his recommendation for Clay Danvers replacement.

Mike turned to his computer and accessed his enormous database. He had access to information on just about everyone. Most people don't realize the vast amount of information that has been collected over the years. Everything has been computerized, from medical records, to shopping habits.

Information is collected everywhere, from the valued customer cards filled out at the grocery store making people eligible for discounts, to the things charged on all forms credit cards. He had meticulously compiled files on everyone he had done business with and practically all government officials he had ties to. He opened the file containing the life and times of Chase Walters and began to prepare a brief for the meeting.

Lawrence stood in the shower letting the water hit him in the face and run down his body. His mind was like a tornado, thoughts and emotions swirling about in his head. He felt alone, confused, and afraid. The stakes had been raised with the death of Clay Danvers. The fact that they were calling it a possible suicide was of little consequence. One way or another, the responsibility for his death was in the hands of one man. He was now confident of the source of the photograph he had received, and its significance was becoming a bit clearer.

Prior to Clay's death, he was prepared to give the Independent Counsel the information he had on Preston Wesley. However, things had changed. In some small way Lawrence felt responsible for Clay's death, much the same way he felt after the death of his wife and son. Only this time, he was not going to sit by and do nothing. This time he would act. He felt guilty coming to this realization only now. He felt like he was cheating his wife and son, rallying only after the death of a man he could at best call a friend.

"Better now than never. Better now than never," he mumbled.

The information he held was enough to bring down the President, but the President was only one man. Clay had said that they know. This meant that there were others, and they had to pay as well. His emotions were now turning to anger. How many lives had to be lost? How many other lives had to be destroyed? He was now pissed. Bringing down Preston Wesley was not enough. He wanted to bring them all down.

Bringing down Wesley was like taking out the local drug pusher, he thought. If you kill one, there will be another one right behind him, eager and ready to supply the never-ending stream of customers. No, he had to go for the heart. He had to go for the source. He had been provided a piece of the puzzle in the form of a photograph. He now believed that this photo contained the players, the significance was a little clearer.

Lawrence had prepared for this day and he appropriately called it D-Day. Over the last year he had established another identity. This identity came with everything he needed to be anonymous. An apartment, cash (no credit cards), identification documents, and even a new wardrobe. He was not sure if he would ever need to use his alter ego. As a matter of fact, he often wondered if he was insane for taking the time and resources to establish it.

In the beginning it was a distraction, a diversion from his troubled life. He had often dreamt of just disappearing. As he reflected, he began to feel a certain sense of relief that his attempt at a distraction was now justified. His reflections brought him to a new realization as well, Kelly. She was not part of this course of action. Sure, the reason he had begun this process was for her, but the situation had taken an unexpected turn, and it was more complex now.

Originally, he was just going to turn over his information to the Independent Counsel and leak portions to the media, but now he would have to go underground. He would have to end it with her and hope that when the dust settled, she would still be there and that she would understand. He could have no ties to her. Nothing could be left of their relationship that could be used to get to him. He couldn't help but feel anxious about letting go of her even if it was only temporary. It had to be, and he went to work on how it would be executed.

# Chapter - - 10

The pressroom in the White House was unusually quiet. Present were the major networks, representatives from the print media, as well as the usual White House press corps. The President had assembled them for a brief statement. No questions would be taken. The room went silent as the Press Secretary for the President, James Montgomery, approached the podium.

"Ladies and gentlemen, thank you for your patience. As I am sure you are aware, this has been a difficult time for the President. He will make a brief statement, and there will be no questions. We will provide you with a written copy of his statement at the conclusion.

"Ladies and gentlemen, the President of the United States."

Everyone in the room was on their feet before James Montgomery had finished introducing the President. As he approached the podium, he motioned for everyone to sit down.

"First, let me begin by thanking each and everyone of you for being here today."

The statement was brief. The funeral would be held at St. Timothy's on Friday. There would be no graveside services, as Clay Danvers had wished to be cremated and his ashes handled by an individual who will not be identified. The President knew who the individual was, and he knew that Clay wished to spend eternity as a part of the mountains he loved so much. That would remain veiled from the public at large out of respect for his friend.

As the reporters filed out, they were given a press packet, which contained the statement read by the President, as well as a bio on Clay Danvers. The President was visibly shaken and vowed to keep alive the memory of his good friend and advisor.

He also promised to pursue the reasons behind the death and asked that the nation join him in becoming involved in lives of those who are close to you. Being involved could circumvent such a tragic and unnecessary end of life. His emotional plea would be the sound bite used by the media at large.

Jason Wheeler had been working non-stop for what seemed like days on the information waxed from the home computer belonging to Lawrence Brazelton. He had gained access to his system and was now cruising through the underbelly of his operating system.

"Sir, I think I have something," he said.

"Let's have it," replied Conner.

"I know how you hate the technical speak, so I will give it to you like this, I found it. You know, the source."

"Just tell me what you found Mr. Wheeler?"

"An obscure mail box. I didn't think it would amount to much but after poking around in it, well…."

Jason paused, and Conner could not tell whether it was out of fright or simple insecurity.

"He has several documents that he has set in an E-mail account as outgoing mail. Apparently, unless he accesses the account once a day and resets the send function by entering his password and moving the time forward, the mail will automatically download and be sent at the time specified."

"What type of documents are we talking about Mr. Wheeler?"

"Have a look. It looks like billing records, as well as legal memos. They have our boys name all over them."

"How did you find this?" Conner asked.

"Hey, it's what you pay me to do. How about a raise?" Jason asked.

"Don't push your luck. You might just ruin my newfound feeling of respect for you. I want copies of those documents PDQ. Then I want you to sit on this until further notice. This info is F.Y.E.O. (for your eyes only). Got it?"

"Yes Sir," he replied.

The laser printer spit out the documents, and Jason handed them to Conner. He disappeared into his makeshift office and scanned them into his laptop. He accessed the Web Page used by the Group for corresponding and attached the documents. Conner had requested hard copies from Jason because he was old fashioned. He liked to keep his own file on any Op they ran, just in case. He hit send and sat back, waiting for his SAT phone to sing its familiar song.


Lawrence was standing in front of the mirror tying his tie when Kelly approached him from behind and put her arms around him.

"That tie looks great."

Lawrence smiled at the compliment. It was refreshing, and one that frankly he had never heard while dressing himself.

"Going somewhere sailor?" she said.

He had planned to become unreasonable, to force an argument in an effort to justify some sort of breakup. He couldn't bring himself to be cruel to her, to hurt her in any way. He knew the next few days would be dangerous for him and potentially bad for her as well. So he decided to be honest.

"We have to talk Kelly," he said.

He motioned for Kelly to sit and so she moved toward the bed and sat on the end with her knees to her chin. Lawrence picked up the remote control, turned on the television, and turned up the volume as he sat next to her. Ever mindful of the possibility that they were being watched and their conversations monitored, he spoke quietly.

"I want you to listen to me and I want you to trust me," he said without looking at her.

"I have to go away for a few days. I want you to trust me and not ask questions."

"I need for you to go and visit you mother. Say she is not well or something. Can you do that for me?" he asked.

"What is wrong? You are scaring me."

"No questions. If you truly love me, you will trust me. All I can say, is that some things have come up, and I need to take care of them. I will explain everything later, I promise."

"But why do I have to leave?" she said as the emotion showed in her voice.

"You just have to, and you just have to trust me. Now, I want you to kiss me goodbye and get yourself together and get out of town. I will be in touch, and we will be together soon, ok?"

As Lawrence stood, he bent over and kissed Kelly. As he began to rise, she grabbed him and hugged him like she was never going to see him again. When she loosened her grip, he stood upright and could see a tear make its way down her cheek. He smiled at her with a look of peace and comfort. She was still holding his hand tightly, but the smile relaxed her grip. Lawrence turned and walked slowly from the bedroom.

Kelly heard the front door close and a moment later the car starting. She felt cold and alone, and it was then she noticed that Lawrence had left his cellular phone on the desk in the bedroom. She leapt from the bed, retrieved it, and ran for the front door. It was too late. He was gone. She stood at the doorway and watched as he turned the corner at the end of the street.

Mike had just finished running the Web Page through the encryption software and was getting his first look at the documents the Dogwatch had uncovered. It was more than he had expected. Lawrence had kept copies of the original records from the firm. The good news was that they had located the information. The bad news was that there was information to uncover. The information revealed a much deeper involvement regarding Preston Wesley. The fact that Lawrence had kept this for so long proved he was willing to use it.

"Never point a loaded gun at someone unless you intend on using it," thought Mike.

This was a loaded gun, and it was apparent that Lawrence was capable of firing it. He printed the information and added it to the brief he had prepared for the Group's meeting later that day. It seemed the group would have a full plate at this meeting with many decisions to make.

In addition to the successor of Clay Danvers and the newly acquired information, was the fact that there was a deep concern for the state of mind of the President. He needed Clay Danvers. Clay was the glue that held this fragile arrangement together.

He had kept the President focused on the greater good. He had packaged the dealings of the Group in a way that kept the President somewhat insulated from them, but at the same time linked like Siamese twins. It was a delicate balance, but it had been carried out flawlessly to this point. Without Clay the President might fold under the pressure and go righteous, as Mike put it. That would be devastating for the Group and political suicide for the President.

He sat and contemplated his next move. He picked up his SAT phone and began punching in numbers. It rang just once.

"Yes?" Conner said.

"Good work Conner. Continue to keep a short leash on Brazelton. I will send you further instructions when I figure out the next move," Mike said.

"Very well," replied Conner.

Mike ended the call with the realization that his next communication with the Dogwatch would be in the form of an order to destroy the source of the information and terminate Lawrence Brazelton.

Lawrence was now in survival mode, ever vigilant of the possibility he was being followed. His first stop would be his office. He would park in the garage, as was normal for him, and spend the morning catching up on his work. During his morning routine, he would inform his secretary that he would be out of the office and unavailable for the following week. His explanation was the need to attend the funeral of his friend and take some time off for his own mental health. This would not seem out of the ordinary for him, due to the fact that since the death of both his wife and son, he had become a slave to his work. It was his way of coping with the emptiness of his life and his home.

Carlos exited the Blazer that he and Victor were driving. He stood on the corner and watched Lawrence pull into the parking garage. He returned to the vehicle and turned his attention to his partner.

"What's the problem?" he said.

"Simple, he left his phone at home," replied Victor.

"Something's not right. He never goes anywhere without that damn phone. We need to put a tag on his car, call Conner," Carlos said.

Victor exited the vehicle and walked briskly to the corner. As he dialed his SAT phone, he kept an eye on the garage, just in case the target decided to leave. The conversation was brief. He returned to the Blazer.

"It's a go," he said.

The garage was large and unattended except for the security guard that patrolled it every hour like clockwork. The parking garage was divided into two somewhat equal halves. One half for visitors and the other half reserved for employees. It was only protected by a swinging arm, which simply required a password to gain access.

Both Carlos and Victor knew that they could access the employee portion with ease. Invariably there was always one employee who feared forgetting their password and would use 1-2-3-4 as a password. It was no exception this time either. They parked, and Victor exited the vehicle with the transmitter in hand. The whole process took less than two minutes.

They returned to their position outside of the office building and began to check to see if the transmitter was sending. Victor turned on his laptop and accessed a tracking program. After typing in the several commands, a map appeared, and in the middle of the screen, they saw a single red dot blinking.

With the up to date maps provided by their employer as well the sophisticated GPS technology, they could track his movements in any city in the world. Victor chuckled out loud at the realization that their maps were probably more up to date than those of the CIA, and their library probably contained even more.

"Bingo," Victor said.

"Houston, we have established contact," he continued.

And now the waiting game had begun.


Lawrence had finished working and was just sitting at his desk twirling a pen between his fingers. The adrenaline was now pumping, as he prepared to leave his current life and begin his new one. As a child, he had dreamed of becoming a super spy, ala James Bond. For the first time since his childhood days, he felt like that dream was becoming a reality.

Only he was more frightened than he could have ever imagined. It was time to go. As he reached the door to his office, he turned for one last look. He switched the lights off, wondering if he would ever be back, wondering if he really cared. After all, this was not his chosen vocation, rather it seemed more like a routine that had no real value or meaning.

His secretary had gone to lunch, so there were no more questions before he left. He snapped his finger as though he had remembered something and returned to his office to retrieve a bag from the bottom of a closet located in his private bathroom.

Making his way past the elevators to the stairs, he descended two flights of stairs to the $7^{th}$ floor and entered a public restroom located next to the stairwell. He had chosen that floor because it was being renovated. The only people around were the construction crews doing the renovations, and they were all on a lunch break as well.

He went into a stall and quickly changed, putting his suit into the bag. As he exited the stall, he stood in front of the mirror to finish his transformation. He then removed a small bottle of glue and added a mustache to his new look. Placing a ball cap on, he looked at the finished product.

Gone was the Armani suit, gold-rimmed Gucci glasses, and Rolex watch. In its place stood a man in jeans, a sweatshirt, windbreaker, ball cap, and black-rimmed glasses.

As he exited the restroom, he passed a chute the workers used for the disposal of construction material. A long silver tube went from the $7^{th}$ floor to a dumpster located in the alley. He pitched the bag in the chute and heard it bang its way down to the street. He made his way to the elevator, then to the lobby, then out the front door.

As he began to make his way down the street, he kept his head down. He turned the corner and passed the Blazer that contained the two members of the Dogwatch. Neither party paid attention to the sequence of events. Lawrence had made his way successfully out of his office, as the two men watched the entrance to the garage waiting to once again tail their mark.

# Chapter - - 11

Old Sam was sitting in the tiny guard shack that he had turned into a home away from home, complete with a TV, coffeemaker and a mini refrigerator. He liked his job, his duties were limited, and his routine was simple. The pay was above scale for someone of his limited background and education. Mr. Baker and the others treated him well, always greeting him warmly and with respect. He never really thought much about what went on in the building.

Only on rare occasions had he even entered it. His main function was to see that nobody ever entered. He would walk the grounds every 45 minutes, check the doors, and chase away the occasional transients or kids that were usually up to no good. Overall, the only person he ever saw on a regular basis was Mr. Baker. No, he never really thought much about anything, until recently. He knew the men that met with Mr. Baker were among the elite in society. He also knew that Mr. Danvers worked for the President. With his recent death and the frequency of the meetings with the other gentlemen, his curiosity was peaking. Then the phone rang.

"Yes Mr. Baker," Sam answered knowing that it was his boss, since he was the only person in the building.

"Sam, Mr. Reyna, Mr. Sullivan, and Mr. Cortina will be arriving shortly. Please know they are expected."

"Yes Mr. Baker. Anything else Sir?"

"No Sam. That will be all. Wait, there is one other thing, after they arrive, why don't you lock it down and go home for the evening."

"Are you sure Sir?"

"Yes I am sure Sam. We will be fine, and you deserve a break."

"Thank you Sir. The misses won't know what to think, me coming home so early and all. She might think I've been fired or something."

"Sam, you haven't been fired. You deserve a break, and we are going to be late. It is as simple as that."

"Well thank you again Mr. Baker Sir. I'll lock her up nice and tight and make my rounds before I go."

"That will be fine Sam. Have a good evening."

Sam sat in the little 4' x 8' room and waited for the arrival of the expected guests. He began to question things, as his curiosity once again took hold. Those thoughts lasted only a moment, as he shrugged them off and went back to watching TV with one ear tuned to his police scanner.

Lawrence had walked for what seemed like hours, ducking in and out of shops, taking a taxi for a few blocks, and constantly checking for someone who was not there. After he began to feel like he was indeed alone, he made his way to his new temporary residence.

As he sat on the second hand sofa, he surveyed his surroundings. It was a simple studio apartment. He had rented it over a year ago, and he had been here only a handful of times. He had explained to the woman who rented it to him that he was a writer and he traveled a great deal. He only needed it for a place to write and spend time when he was in town. She didn't seem to mind since he paid 18 months rent in advance as well as the ridiculous security deposits she had demanded.

He slowly got up, his knees and back cracking and popping. It was the result of a day spent wandering the street trying to evade an enemy who had yet to realize that Lawrence Brazelton was even missing. He half walked and half limped to the small desk that faced the window.

Everything was covered with a fine layer of dust that showed there had been no one present for some time. On the desk sat a laptop computer, a scanner, and a multi purpose printer. Lawrence bent over to plug it in, then powered it up. He had two purposes, locate the golf course in the photo and reset his E-mail account. He first accessed his mail account and reset the system. He felt better having accomplished that simple task. He was not ready for that information to be made public just yet.

Next, he removed a newspaper from the backpack he had used in place of his briefcase and retrieved the photograph that he now knew Clay Danvers had sent him. He laid it on the desk and began studying it. He sat and stared at it, standing several times with his hand on his chin, only to sit back down. Then he saw it.

It was now past 5:00pm. Carlos and Victor began to wonder where Lawrence was. As the steady stream of cars exiting the garage became more of a trickle, their concerns grew. Both men stared intently at the computer screen and in particular the single red dot flashing steadily on the screen, it had not moved.

"I guess the only question is, who's gonna check out his office?" said Carlos.

"I'll check out the garage. You check the office," replied Victor.

"Man that sucks. You always get the easy shit," Carlos said.

"Intelligence has its privileges my young friend," Victor said, as he was halfway out the door.

Carlos watched as Victor made his way across the street and disappeared into the garage. He waited, and then he exited and made his way across the street and entered the front entrance to the office building. Carlos walked briskly towards the elevator passing the security guard's desk, as if he knew exactly where he was going and what he was doing. He knew that he stood a better chance of not being questioned if he looked as if he had a purpose and lacked the need for assistance. Apparently it worked, because the security guard had just looked up briefly and then went back to reading his Sports Illustrated.

The doors of the elevator opened to the 9th floor, and Carlos exited. There were only two office suites on the 9th floor, and both seemed to be empty. He made his way towards Brazelton's office. No one seemed to be there. He tried the door and found that it was locked. He moved from in front of the large glass front entry, removed his SAT phone, and quickly dialed Brazelton's private line. Peaking around and peering through the glass, he waited for Lawrence to answer. There was no movement, and no one answered the phone.

Carlos waited for another moment. Satisfied that the office was empty, he made his way back to the Blazer. Victor was waiting for him.

"The car is still in the garage, and the transmitter is still in place."

"Nobody is in the office."

Victor looked down and shook his head.

"The boss is gonna be pissed, big time," he said as he began to dial his phone.

"Yes?" Conner said as he answered the phone.

"Birds flown. He is in the open," Victor said.

"Come home," Conner replied.

Victor slammed the phone on the dash and barked at Carlos to drive. Both men knew that no matter how calm the boss sounded on the phone, reality was a different story. The ride back to the command center was painfully silent.

Conner was in fact pissed. However, he was a professional and in his line of work, shit happens. Sometimes it was sweet and sometimes it stunk to high heaven. This time it stunk. He wondered if the death of Clay Danvers had spooked Lawrence. They had what they wanted, the information that their employer had requested. Maybe that would be enough. No, he knew better than that. He knew that if there were copies in some E-mail account, that there was a possibility that the originals were out there somewhere. He also knew that Lawrence was a threat himself and that the order would come to eliminate him the same way they had eliminated so many others. It was time to inform his employer. The only question was, did he feel like writing it or saying it. He looked at his computer, and then he looked at his phone.

He didn't have to think long, as he was already punching in the numbers on his SAT phone. Conner never dodged a confrontation.

"Yes Mr. Braxton?" Mike said as he answered the phone.

"I am sorry to report that the subject is in the open."

"What!"

"We trailed him to his office. The boys got a little concerned when he left his home this morning without his phone. They called it in and requested to put a transmitter on the car. At some point during the day, he simply walked off."

"Let me congratulate you on locating the information. However, let me remind you that losing him is unacceptable. We need to locate this man, and I mean now!"

"Yes Sir."

"Let me remind you that the information was being held electronically, which means that there is a possibility that the originals are still out there."

"Yes Sir."

"What do you think made him run?" asked Mike.

"The death of Mr. Danvers would be my guess," replied Conner.

"It is not important to list the reasons why. Just find him. I am sending you a nice little package, so check your E-mail. Please see that Mr. Wheeler puts it to good use, and keep me informed as to your progress in locating our lost pigeon."

"Yes Sir," replied Conner.

Conner sat in the silence of his makeshift office, which felt more like home than did his own home. Why he had a home was anybody's guess. He spent the majority of his time traveling and sleeping in makeshift accommodations. Buying the house had provided him with a sense of stability and belonging, something he longed for.

His thoughts drifted from the sublime to his current situation. He couldn't help but feel a certain antipathy for his employer. He hated to hear that which was common sense thrown back in his face like a child. That, however, was the employee / employer relationship. So, he checked his E-mail for the package that was promised by his employer.

Lawrence could not believe that it had taken him so long to see what was now staring him in the face. Preston Wesley was even standing next to it. He quickly scanned the photo into his computer and highlighted the sign located at the tee box. He enlarged the highlighted area.

*Rivermont Country Club*
*15th hole, Par 4, 375 yards*

Rivermont was an exclusive Country Club in the rolling hills of West Virginia. It was home to people who wanted to shoot a round of golf in peace, quiet, and anonymity. Getting on the course would not be easy. Large stonewalls surrounded it and the only access was through the front gate. A security guard watched the gate, and the only way to gain access was with a scheduled tee time. This was a luxury afforded to members and their guests. Lawrence met neither of those criteria.

The grounds were patrolled on a regular basis 24 hours a day. This was in large part due to the exclusive and eccentric nature of the club's members. To shoot a round of golf at Rivermont was to be completely comfortable and secure. Leaders of countries, industry, celebrities, and visiting dignitaries frequented the course. Lawrence sat back in his chair and looked up at the ceiling, eyes closed and mouth wide open. How was a man who was trying to be anonymous, trying not to stand out, going to pull this off?

As the last of Mr. Baker's guests arrived, Sam locked down the garage and began to walk the perimeter of the building. He stopped at every door checking to make sure that it was secure. He scanned the property surrounding the structure for anything that seemed out of place. Sam was a company man through and through, and he carried out his duties without question and to the letter.

He felt comfortable with his efforts and walked briskly to his car. Opening the door, he stepped in and drove off, watching the building slowly grow smaller in his rear view mirror. He began again to be somewhat curious but pushed the questions aside, he was not the type to get involved. He just wanted to put in his time and retire to Florida, spend time drinking, fishing, and telling tall tales. Yes, that's what appealed to Sam, and that's why he couldn't afford to be concerned.

Mike Baker stood in front of the large picture window in the conference room where the Group conducted its meetings. The room was eerily quiet and filled with a certain sense of fear and uncertainty. Mike chaired the meeting as usual, and all eyes were glued to him waiting in anticipation for him to speak. Time seemed to stand still, as what was merely a few seconds, seemed in fact to be pain-filled hours.

He slowly turned in a dramatic fashion as he was accustomed to, and faced the other members.

"Gentlemen, please open the information packets in front of you," he said.

"As you can see, we have a great deal of information to disseminate over the course of this little get together, so I would ask for your patience."

" Item number one on the list, Mr. Brazelton has eluded our watch team and is now in the open. The only positive thing I can glean from this unfortunate turn of events is that our team has discovered the nature and the location of the information that Mr. Brazelton has in his possession. You will find copies of the documents in your portfolios. As you can see, the information is substantial, as well as damning. My main, I am sorry, our main concern should be the existence of any hard copies of that information."

"Mike, what exactly do we do?" asked Patrick.

"You do nothing. I have instructed our team to terminate the source of the electronic information, as well as see to the ultimate capture of Mr. Brazelton for possible retrieval of any further information. If he has gone missing, we may as well use it to our advantage."

"Do you think that is wise?" asked Neil.

"It may not be wise, however, it is prudent," replied Mike.

"Next on the agenda is the issue of who we shall tap as a replacement for Mr. Danvers. As you are painfully aware, we need someone close to the President, someone with whom he has the utmost respect for as well as someone who sees this country the same way we do."

"And how is that Mike? As a fat cow that needs milking?" Bart Sullivan commented sarcastically.

Mike let the question hang in the air before answering, partly to make Bart feel uncomfortable and in part to show who dictated the flow of the conversation.

"We may not always agree on the ultimate direction and purpose of this body. However, you have gained and profited from your participation. All of you have advanced many of your pet projects and concerns as well. So let us not lose our focus. Whether you decide to use your membership in our organization for profit, power, or a clear conscience, a need for a replacement still exists."

"You are so painfully right. You are an asshole, but your right. So tell us, who has your little computer chosen for the task at hand?" replied Bart.

"Very clever Mr. Sullivan. After a good deal of research, as well as careful consideration, I feel our best option for recruitment would be Chase Walters."

He carefully watched each member of the Group as they turned to look at each other as if someone had to say something.

"The President's Chief of Staff?" exclaimed Bart.

"Have you lost your mind? Are you nuts?" he continued.

"Like I said, after a great deal of research and consideration, that is the conclusion I have come to."

"What makes you think he would consider the dark nature of our arrangement? Or better yet, what makes you think he would even be remotely interested?" Neil asked.

Mike was noticeably irritated by the tone of the questions and by the sheer fact that he had to explain himself. Staying focused and keeping his composure, he continued.

"There are two reasons to why Mr. Walters will choose to join our little group. The first is of course money and the second is the need to keep secrets. Everyone has something to hide. Our Mr. Walters is no exception."

"Why him, and more importantly who is going to initiate contact with him?" asked Patrick.

"You need not worry, any of you. I will handle the recruitment of Mr. Walters. I would not want any of you to dirty those pretty little hands any more than is necessary. As for my reasons, they are simple. He has an inside track to the next administration, as well as the ear of the President."

"If there are no further questions or objections, I would like to continue."

The tone of his voice was slowly changing. The irritation of being second-guessed and questioned was emerging. He paused in an effort to regain his composure.

"As for the funeral of Mr. Danvers, I recommend that we, individually, do not attend. Furthermore, until the Brazelton matter is dealt with, I recommend that we limit any further meetings. Any and all communications shall be conducted via our secure data resources. Enclosed within your packets is the latest version of a new encryption program I have designed. This software will update the existing program on your personal computers, as well as your PDA, once downloaded and synced. Please see to it at your earliest possible convenience. If there are no other issues at hand, I would ask for an adjournment at this time."

Mike looked at each member of the Group waiting for someone to speak. No one did. He was grateful because he was losing control, not control of the meeting, but control of the situation. That irritated him most of all. Control was everything to Mike Baker.

"Very well then. Please review the information I have provided you. Inside you will also find copies of our financial status as a group, as well as all pending legislation that pertains to this body. Please see to it that you continue to engage in your roles and that you protect the interests of this body. Thank you, and good night."

Mike turned to face the window once again as the other members of the Group gathered their material and exited the conference room. He could not help but feel the looks of the other members as they left. Like lasers, they seemed to burn through the back of his head. He knew that he might have stepped out of line, taken too much of a leadership role. The Group was in theory made up of equal parts, but Mike was not one to stand idly by and play a passive role in anything. Besides, someone always had to lead.

Lawrence was lying on the bed in the opposite corner of the studio apartment from his desk. He had arranged it that way so that the bed was as far away from the window as possible. His thoughts drifted towards Kelly. He missed her smell, her touch, and her presence. He wondered what she was doing right now. He hoped she had listened to his admonitions, and he wondered if she missed him as much as he missed her. His thoughts began to float back in time to a place he rarely visited because the pain was still deep and fresh.

Memories of life at home and at the office flooded his mind like a raging river. He remembered when he first had a need to learn about computers. It was an average day at the office, and he needed access to a file. It was a simple enough task. However, on that particular day his legal assistant, Stacy, was out of the office. He boldly walked to her desk and turned on the computer, thinking that a man as intelligent as he was could retrieve the information with ease.

How wrong he was. He felt like he was in a foreign country, in a land that spoke an all too different language. He fumbled with the keys and the messages on the screen to no avail.

He recalled the frustration he felt and the powerlessness and lack of skill. That very evening he went home and grabbed his wife, and they purchased their first computer. By today's standards, that computer was a dinosaur. It was a 386DX with 4 Megs of Ram, a 800MB hard drive, and a 2500bps modem. At the time, it was the racehorse and envy of his neighbors.

As these memories floated through his mind, he glanced at the laptop on the small desk opposite of him and smiled. He had taught himself everything he knew about computers. He had hated the feeling of being helpless, of needing someone else to handle such a simple task. Now he could not only retrieve files, he was a day trader on the stock market. He did his checking online, and he was savvy enough to store his life insurance policy on it.

Conner sat in his office and reviewed the package sent to him by his employer. Contained within were the instructions to locate and terminate Lawrence Brazelton and if possible locate the existence of any hard copies of his information. The first order of business, however, was to take down the electronic source of his information.

His employer had sent along a program that contained a virus. This virus when introduced to the server that held Brazelton's information would act as a worm virus. It would destroy the information contained in his personal mailbox and it would then automatically send itself to any address contained in his mail account.

Once inside, the worm would effectively erase his hard drive, as well as any computer he communicated with. The key, as with any virus, was to get Lawrence to actually open an E-mail in which it was contained. Under normal circumstances that might have been a problem, however, they had access to his account now. They could introduce the virus by pretending to be Lawrence accessing his mail account remotely.

Conner was about to break ranks. He wanted Lawrence first, and then he would take down the information. He had been doing black Ops since his employer was pimple faced and playing arcade games with his geek friends. He knew that if they were to remove his trump card, it would serve only to drive him under deeper than ever. No, he would use the information to smoke him out. But first he would have to talk to Jason to figure out exactly how that would occur. He quickly burned a copy of the virus to a CD and placed it in a jewel case.

Mike was busy doing what he loved, playing with his computer. It was his way of relaxing, and it had made him billions as well. He bounced in and out of servers all over the world, making it all but impossible to trace the source of the message he was sending. This particular message was very important. It was directed to who he hoped was a new friend. As he cleared the last hurdle, the Presidential Seal appeared on his screen.

Armed with the necessary passwords and E-mail address, he finished his work and exited the system. He leaned back in his chair with a tremendous look of satisfaction on his face. He had finished his work for the day, and for the first time in two days he prepared to go home for a good night's rest. He had to get up early for his appointment tomorrow.

Chase Walters was preparing to leave for the evening. He was about to get up when the indicator sounded, informing him that he had mail. He set down his briefcase and pointed his mouse at the small envelope in the lower left hand corner of the screen. The screen went to black for only a split second, then a picture began to slowly descend down the screen. Chase sat back with his eyes wide open and then his jaw dropped.

He quickly spun around to make sure no one was in his office looking over his shoulder. Turning again to face the monitor he was stunned. There on the screen was a picture of him with Rachel. He had been seeing Rachel for sometime, but had recently broken it off. Rachel was what one might call a working girl. Chase had begun this tawdry affair during a rough spot in his otherwise happy marriage.

Afraid to move, frozen by fear and paranoia, he just stared. After what seemed like an eternity, he gathered his senses and scrolled down past the picture and an audio message box appeared. He hit the play button.

What he heard made his stomach clench. It was a brief recording of him bragging to this prostitute about his work at the White House, along with the fact that he allowed her to listen to conversations between he and the President. As the recording ended, he continued to scroll down and he found the text of the message.

*"Now that I have your attention, let me assure you that my intentions are honorable. I have no interest in this information going any further than this. I would like to invite you to join me for a round of golf tomorrow at 9:00am at the Rivermont Country Club. You are expected and will be welcomed at the gate and directed where to go from there."*

*A new friend!*

Chase continued to stare at the monitor. He knew that secrets were a rare commodity in Washington, and they always had a way of falling out of the closet. But this, this was no skeleton simply falling out. As the fear and sickness began to subside, he began to mumble the words of the text.

"Honorable intentions?"

"Information going no further than this?"

"Signed, a new friend?"

If someone had wanted him out, they would have simply leaked it to the press. But they hadn't. Instead, they wanted to golf, and at the most exclusive course in the country. He began to ease up a bit and realized this was about business. But who was this so-called new friend? He would not have to wait long to find out. He deleted the mail from his computer.

Normally he would have had the Secret Service trace the origin of the message. Unauthorized access to the White House system was extremely rare, but an offense nonetheless. This was no normal situation, and he did not want to share this portion of his life with the Secret Service. He picked up his briefcase, turned out the lights, and began the mental preparations for his meeting with his new friend.

# Chapter - - 12

Mike Baker had no need for an alarm clock. His was a fine-tuned mixture of body and mind. His biological clock would wake him at 4:30 every morning regardless of the time he retired the previous evening. This morning was no exception, and he awoke refreshed and ready for the day.

As was customary, he crossed his bedroom to his elaborate office located just off of the master suite. Waiting for him was a tray containing his morning coffee, an English muffin, and several of the morning papers. He poured his coffee and put honey on both halves of the muffin. Reaching forward, he turned on his computer and proceeded to sit down. He began as usual by reading the newspaper.

The newspaper was the only form of media he read that was actually on paper. He could not seem to give up the feel and the smell of a freshly printed newspaper. Maybe it went back to the early days of his youth and the fact that a paper route was his first source of income. Everything was digital in nature, except the morning paper, and even they were selling out to the digital age. His excitement for the day's events prevented him from enjoying his normal morning routine.

He pushed the papers aside and went directly into his personal Web Page. That page was comprised of shortcuts to his mail account, the encrypted Web Page he used for information transfers to the Dogwatch, as well as links to the stock market and business clippings from the wire services. This morning he was interested in only one thing. What new information had developed overnight regarding Lawrence Brazelton?

As the Web Page began its encryption process, Mike watched the screen. It transformed and displayed the same content that was there yesterday. This meant that there was no new information. He began to wonder if Conner had followed directions and taken down the server containing the condemning information regarding Preston Wesley.

He began to type a message to Conner, then stopped. He would let it be until the end of the day. He had other pressing matters and did not want to spoil the good mood he had found himself in this particular morning. There was something about corrupting people that gave him a certain sense of satisfaction. Maybe it was the power, the ability to compromise someone, to change them, and make them a useful pawn in his twisted game. Regardless of the reasons, he retired to the bathroom to prepare himself for the day.

Lawrence had had a rough night. It started in the bed and ended on the sofa. The television had remained on the entire night. Lawrence was not sure when exactly it was that he was able to achieve sleep, if you could even call it that. He moved about the small studio apartment and began to brew his morning elixir, a special blend of exotic Java.

Coffee was the one vice he had, and it had become somewhat of a holy grail in his morning ritual. As he sat at his desk, he began to contemplate his strategy for the day. He knew that he would have to make his way to Rivermont Country Club. He knew he had to find a way to make it inside the exclusive resort, but how? His mind was spinning. He couldn't think until he had his first cup of coffee. He was not a morning person, and he hadn't been for several years.

He remembered when he couldn't wait to hit the bricks in the morning. The excitement of a new day was like the smell of the air after an afternoon rain, cool and refreshing. Now he loathed each new day. The thought of one more day in this piece of shit world depressed him. His coffee was finishing its final drip as he retrieved the pot and poured himself a tall one. No sugar and no cream today, straight and black. As was customary, the day began to take on a bit more light with each sip of his coffee, the loathing dissipated and the hope returned.

He laughed inside at the thought that this was one powerful legal stimulant. If the government ever decided to attack the coffee lobby, America would be thrust into a civil war. With his head now a bit clearer, he picked up the yellow pages and began an earnest search for a car rental company. Not the mainstream companies. He needed a company that took cash and didn't ask many questions. He found what appeared to be the place.

"Lucky's Rentown."

That was the ticket. He threw on a pair of jeans, a cap, and his glasses. He gathered his laptop, and shot out the door. After taking 2 buses and several taxis, careful to watch his back, Lawrence arrived at the Lucky's Rentown. He wandered the lot and looked at every car available. He was careful not to choose a car that would look too out of place in the exclusive Rivermont area. After several minutes and no luck, a man approached him.

"Good morning Sir, and what a fine morning it is, if I can say so. The name is Lucky. What can I do ya for?"

One thing that Lawrence possessed that had served him well as an attorney was his ability to recognize less than reputable individuals. Lucky, it appeared, was just that. Individuals like Lucky could get you anything you wanted, provided you spoke his language, the language of money, cold hard cash.

"Listen, I need a car. Only I prefer to drive something with a little more style, if you know what I mean?" Lawrence began.

"Well Sir, what you see is what you get," replied Lucky.

"Now if you want a Jag, Mercedes, or a Porsche, I can direct you to a great place just down the street a bit," he continued.

Lawrence took a wad of bills from his pocket and held it in the palm of his hand as he spoke.

"I was sure hoping you could assist me. You see I need a car, only for a day but I have an aversion to filling out paperwork. All those formalities you know, it makes me feel uneasy. Naturally, I would be willing to pay for the benefit of foregoing all of those formalities," Lawrence said as he toyed with the wad of cash in his hand.

Lucky stood there for a moment, looking around as if he was waiting for someone to walk up and yell, gottcha. He rubbed his hands together and then suddenly clapped and said.

"I understand completely. Why don't you step into my office. I think I can assist you. Here at Lucky's Rentown our number one priority is to give the customer what they want."

Lawrence followed his newfound friend to an office located behind a locked gate. Once inside the office, Lucky began to enter information into his computer. He turned the monitor around so that Lawrence could see it.

"As you can see, we have several vehicles that should please a man of your obvious tastes and style."

Lawrence looked at the screen and there were indeed several beautiful automobiles. He figured they were stolen and that they had had the registrations altered, and were probably located somewhere close.

"I will take that one," Lawrence indicated.

"Mercedes, nice choice. Our going rate for that particular car is $2,000 a day. That is, of course, cash paid in advance."

"Of course," replied Lawrence.

Lawrence counted out the money and handed it to Lucky, who again counted it. After being satisfied that the amount was correct, he picked up the phone and rattled off some numbers.

"Can I get you a complimentary cup of coffee while you wait?" asked Lucky.

"Sure," came the reply.

After about 20 minutes and two cups of coffee that could be best described as mud, a slender man appeared and handed Lucky a set of keys. Lucky turned to Lawrence and handed them to him. True to his word, Lawrence was pulling out of the lot, no questions asked. He made his way down the city streets towards the parkway. Still careful and somewhat paranoid, he took a round-about way, checking the mirrors every few seconds. Satisfied he was not being followed, he entered the parkway and headed for Rivermont.

Chase Walters had not slept at all that night. He was agitated and short tempered with his wife and housekeeper. He had phoned the White House earlier to inform his assistant that he would not be in until later that day. He had some unscheduled things arise overnight and would require some time to see to them today.

Luckily, his new friend had picked a slow day at the White House for their rendezvous. Chase was short with his assistant as he began to ask too many questions. He told the little shit if he ever expected to be anything other than an assistant, he would have to learn to handle unexpected events. His morning was not going well. He had dismissed his government driver and was now on his way to meet with his new friend. He had not driven in sometime and was amazed at how nervous he was behind the wheel.

Lawrence sat in a parking lot that he thought probably belonged to the employees of the Rivermont Country Club. It was approximately 50 yards from the gated entrance to the exclusive resort. He had a clear view of the front gate. He reached into his backpack and produced a pair of very small field binoculars. He sat back and began to watch the comings and goings at the main gate.

Field intelligence and observation was unfamiliar to him. He was not sure what he was hoping to accomplish or what he was hoping to see. Even if he did see something, would he even know of its significance? He noted that as a car approached, its occupants were greeted at the gate by what looked like a caddy and a security officer.

The security officer held a wand out and appeared to be sweeping for bugs and possibly weapons, Lawrence imagined. During that process, the caddy was busy loading the clubs onto the golf cart. After the cursory inspection, the caddy drove them through the gate. The member's car was then taken to another parking lot located on the opposite side of the street from the entrance by a valet.

Lawrence watched this ritual for several minutes when suddenly one of the men from the photograph emerged from his car at the gate. He quickly dug into his backpack and removed the photo to make certain he hadn't been mistaken. He was not. As the man exited his vehicle, he appeared to look around as if he were expecting someone. After a few moments, he sat in the golf cart and was driven through the gates by his caddy. Rather than a valet parking his car, his personal driver parked the vehicle.

Shortly after the arrival of Mike Baker, another vehicle approached the front gate. It was Chase Walters. The President's Chief of Staff exited the vehicle and was led through the same procedure. Lawrence did not need a photograph to recognize Walters. What caught Lawrence by surprise was that Walters had driven himself, something no high level hotshot does. There was no Secret Service and no government driver.

That in and of its self triggered the bells and whistles that were now ringing in the ears of Lawrence Brazelton. Why would the President's Chief of Staff enter an exclusive Country Club without the accompaniment of a driver and or protection? And why would the timing of the arrival of Mike Baker and Chase Walters be so close? He asked himself these questions, but he already knew the answer, power meeting power. The phrase on the back of the photo was playing loudly in his head.

"He who has all the gold makes the rules."

He had just watched the richest man in the world, as well as one of the closest men to the President, enter an exclusive Country Club virtually at the same time. Was it a coincidence? That was possible, but not likely. He knew now more than ever that he had to find out what Clay had left inside that Country Club. He laid the binoculars on the seat and started the car.


Mike was waiting on the first tee taking some practice swings as Chase approached. He was comfortable with his decision to meet Chase Walters at Rivermont, because prior to entering the Country Club each person was swept for bugs or recording devices of any kind. This was done in an effort to relieve the anxiety of its members and fostered an atmosphere of complete confidence.

Mike handed his caddy his club and told him that they would be walking this morning and would not need the golf carts. He approached Chase with his hand extended and a grand smile on his face. He removed the large Cuban Cigar he was smoking and spoke.

"Thank you for accepting my invitation. A glorious morning is it not?"

"Your invitation? Is that what you call an invitation?"

"My dear man, had I simply asked you to join me, there would have been secretaries and schedules involved. Conflicts over acceptable times would have come up, and who knows, we may have gotten around to this meeting in early spring."

"Maybe that's the problem. Normal people do at least ask."

"I meant what I said. The information contained in my communication was mere motivation and not for public consumption."

"Enough with the semantics. What is the purpose of this meeting?"

"I want the company of a fellow warrior for the pleasure of 18 holes of golf, during which we can discuss certain issues that we have in common."

Chase looked at the man with penetrating eyes, and he realized that he had little choice in the matter. Washington was anything but kind in the arena of public opinion regarding issues of morality. Sure his President had survived the scandals of having sexual exploits. However, such fortunes were never the case for individuals such as he. No, society was not anxious to cut off the head. They could sacrifice the other extremities, but not the head.

"As the guest, you have honors," Mike said.

Chase took a few moments to warm up and stretch his tired body. The lack of sleep didn't help matters, and it was evident when his tee shot sliced badly.

"Tough break Chase. I can call you Chase?"

"Shit! And it is Mr. Walters to you!" Chase said in disgust as he threw his club towards his caddy almost hitting the man.

Without responding to the outburst by Chase, Mike eyed his ball as it lay on the tee and swung through the ball driving it straight down the fairway. After instructing both caddies to follow at a comfortable distance, he began to make his pitch to Chase.

"The information I share with you today, I share in confidence. I expect this conversation is to remain as private as you expect your extra curricular activities to remain. If you decide to talk and share this with anyone, I will first deny any such meeting ever took place. Then you will meet with an unfortunate accident, or perhaps maybe someone close to you will," Mike stated.

"Are you threatening me? Are you threatening my family? Do you realize that threatening a government official is a federal offense?" Chase replied.

"People such as myself do not threaten. That is such a barbaric term. We simply convey proper motivation in an effort to ensure a basic understanding. Besides, you know how I do business. It was not so long ago that you took my money in trade for services rendered."

"That was in a different life and completely above board. It was business, plain and simple."

"This is business as well my friend. After all, politicians are employees hired to work for their boss, the people. I am pretty sure I qualify as a person, so in fact you do work for me, once again. And as you know, I always get what I want."

Chase stopped abruptly and turned to look at Mike Baker. The caddies, who were following at a comfortable distance stopped as well. What Chase saw in the eyes of his companion sent chills up his spine, and simultaneously, the hairs on the back of his neck began to rapidly stand on end. His eyes were that of a stone cold killer and a man who meant what he said. He knew then and there that his new friend could quickly and without warning become his new enemy given the chance. Without speaking, he turned and began to walk again. After a few steps, he spoke, this time with the tone of a defeated man.

Mike listened and was pleased that his message had been received. He now had the full attention of his prey. Mike made his pitch and as they made the turn for the back nine, the Group had a new member. His name was Chase Walters, and the conversion was far less painful than either man had anticipated.

# Chapter - - 13

Lawrence found himself driving around the immediate vicinity of the Country Club. He was comfortable knowing that he was not drawing attention to himself, and felt somewhat safe in the confines of the Mercedes Benz with dark tinted windows. He was looking for anything that appeared to be an opening, anything that would gain him access to Rivermont. He had circled the perimeter of the massive Country Club.

An immense wall wormed its way around its borders protecting the monolith. He noticed that the wall ended at the shores of a large lake, on the back end of what appeared to be the front nine, and picked up again somewhere around the second hole of the back nine.

He was now parked in a neighborhood directly across the lake from the Country Club. He drove the streets, winding through the exclusive lakeside community, and happened upon a house that appeared to be vacant with a "For Sale" sign in the front yard. He pulled the car into the large circular driveway. As he exited the car, he looked around, still somewhat paranoid of being followed. Peering through the windows he discovered that the home was not occupied at the present. He made his way to the side of the home and through a gate located between the garage and the main house.

Standing in the backyard, he surveyed his surroundings noting that the yard was impressive. What caught his attention was the ramp leading to a small dock at the lakeside. He walked down the ramp and was now standing on the dock looking across the lake at the golf course.

Tethered to the dock was a small sailboat and another small boat, which looked like a cross between a canoe and a rowboat. He looked again across the lake and then again at the two boats. He had found his opening. He stood on the dock enjoying the crisp clear air. In the warm glow of the late morning sun, he began to formulate his strategy.

He knew that he would have to establish the routine of the guards. Learn how many there were in the evenings, etc. That would require him to return to the city and meet with Lucky to see about renting the car for a few days more. Something was exciting about all this, he thought. He turned to make his way to the car for the trip back to the city. He wanted to hurry so he could return again that evening. He had other items to pick up, and he felt time was of the essence.

Mike waited for his driver at the entrance to Rivermont, and he could not hold back the smile that washed over his face. He loved his life. He loved the power he possessed, and he loved the game. Mike viewed everything as a game. In a game there had to be a winner and a loser. That environment and thought process fostered the competition he craved. He reflected on the day's events, on how he had so eloquently and persuasively handled Chase Walters.

Mike was a master at reading and exploiting the weakness of his prey. It was what had made him the man he was today. Chase was a man who was no different than any of the other men that were part of the beltway gang.

When people first hit the beltway, they come full of idealistic dreams of doing good, making things right, and building a greater nation. This was recognized as a rookie mentality, Chase Walters was no rookie. He had spent what seemed to be a lifetime as one of the beltway insiders, including the time he worked for Mike back in the old days.

Once inside and exposed to the money and power, he soon fell victim to its lure. Much like a drug addict will tell you of their downward spiral into a life of hopeless addiction trying to obtain the feelings and sensations of their first high, the same was true of politics. Once an individual witnessed and tasted the sensations of what money and power offered, they had to have more. They had to feed the addiction.

Mike had nailed it. Chase Walters was addicted to the lure and sensation of his lifestyle and would do whatever it took to not only maintain it, but to expand it. He would be a nice addition to the Group and a definite improvement over Clay Danvers. He had the ear of the President on a daily basis.

As a matter of common insider knowledge, it was even known that he was the one that made policy. Whenever faced with a tough question or position, the President would defer to Chase and almost always go with his opinions and in his direction. Naturally, this was more of a choreographed dance than outright deferral and acceptance.

Typically, when faced with a somewhat difficult situation, the President would merely ask for Chase's opinion on the matter, and then after what would appear to be careful consideration, utter the same opinion as if it were his own. Now the opinion of the Group would garner much more favor in the decisions of not only the current President, but possibly for the next two administrations as well. This pleased Mike greatly.

As his driver opened the door, Mike activated his PDA and sent a message to the other members of the Group informing them of the new addition. As he hit the send button, he told the driver to take him to his office. He then booted up his laptop. His car was a well-equipped mobile office. Everything he needed to conduct business was at his disposal. Mike often said that it was a four-wheel version of Air Force One.

Wireless technology made faxing, talking, and surfing the net a mobile affair. He was anxious to check on the progress of the Dogwatch. Technology was wonderful, he thought, as he connected to the Internet and accessed the homepage that they used to communicate.

He watched the page go through its transformation as the encryption program deciphered it. He was troubled by the fact the page had not been updated. That meant that there was no new news regarding Lawrence Brazelton. Which also meant that no progress had been made. Irritated by this, Mike terminated his Internet connection and began punching numbers on the keypad of his SAT phone.

"Yes?" Conner answered.

"What do I pay you fools for? With everything you have at your disposal, you can't provide me with anything that resembles progress? I am headed for the office, and I want a status report up and available for my viewing. And you better have something that is worth my time and my considerable contributions to you! Do you understand me?"

"Yes," came the single word response from Conner.

As Mike disconnected the call, he found that his mood had gone from one of smug satisfaction to one of extreme unhappiness and dissatisfaction. His recruitment of Chase Walters would be of little consequence if the administration were to suffer at the hands of Lawrence Brazelton. He had to be stopped.

Conner sat in his office. He was not used to being chastised like a child. He had flashes of strangling Mike Baker with his bare hands, watching the life leave his body. At the same time he to was angry, angry for having lost control of the situation. How did a wormy suit better his men? Maybe Baker was right. Maybe they should take out the source of Lawrence's information. He reclined back in his chair and stared at the ceiling wondering what to do.

First things first, he had to get a status report from the team and begin to formulate something that resembled a status report for his employer. Gathering several pieces of paper and stuffing them into a folder, he made his way out the door and into the outer room. Jason was hunched over his computer, and the other members of his team were sitting off to the side playing cards.

"Gentlemen, let's get it together," Conner said as he headed for the large folding table that served as a conference table.

"And that includes you Wheeler. Now!"

After the members of the team had settled in their chairs, Conner began.

"I just got off the phone with the man who pays the bills, and let me tell you he is not pleased. He is expecting a status report that contains substance as well as progress, so here is what I want ladies."

"Wheeler, I want a run down on where we are on the techno front. Can we use the system for possibly locating the target? And what, if any, activity has been reported on credit cards, ATM cards, etc?"

"Carlos, Victor, I want you to return to his office. I want to know what happened. Did he leave with someone? Did he leave on his own? How did he manage to get past you? Check the security cameras in the adjacent buildings, ask questions, and find me something."

"Nathan, I want you to hit his house. Retrieve all the hardware we left, and do a hard target search of the premises. See if we missed something. I want you all back here by 1600 hours. Is that clear?"

"Yes Sir," they said collectively.

"Very well then. What are you waiting for, an engraved invitation? Hit the bricks!" Conner said.

With that, he once again gathered up his paperwork and headed for his office, this time closing the door with a little more enthusiasm than usual.


Lawrence pulled into Lucky's Rentown lot and was greeted by Lucky, who asked him to please wait in the car and drive it through the rear gate after he opened it.

Once inside, Lucky greeted him with a warm smile and a handshake.

"I hope you enjoyed your driving experience," Lucky said.

"I did indeed. However, I would like to discuss the terms for an extended period of time," Lawrence said.

"And exactly how long are we talking?" replied Lucky.

"How about an additional two days?"

"I am sure we can come to some sort of arrangement."

"Excellent. The same rate I assume?"

"I think we can offer you a little better rate than that. We do tend to take care of our valued return customers."

"I was wondering if you could help me out in obtaining a few additional items as well?" Lawrence asked.

"I can get you practically anything you need," replied Lucky.

Lawrence handed Lucky a hastily written list of items that he was interested in.

"How late are you open?" Lawrence asked.

"How late do you need me to be open?" Lucky replied

"Would around 7:00pm be alright?"

"That would be fine," he said.

"I will pay you for the vehicle and the items on the list when I return," Lawrence said.

"See you at seven," Lucky said as Lawrence made his way out the gate.

Lucky waited until Lawrence had exited the gate and began to go over the items on the list. He did not see a problem in obtaining any of the items that his new friend and client had requested. As a matter of fact, he had been required to obtain far more difficult things in the past for his many other clients. Lucky liked to think of his marks as clients. It made him feel somewhat legitimate and respectable. As he looked at the list, he read each item off individually:

*Binoculars (high power)*
*Night vision scope or goggles*
*Small shovel*
*Flashlight*
*2 Electric trolling motors, charged*
*.45-caliber semi automatic w/ box of shells*
"Piece of cake," he muttered.

Lawrence made his way back to his apartment. The woman who had rented the room to him peered through the drapes as he made his way up the steps. He could tell she was still trying to figure him out. He did look very different from the first time they had met. He waived at her and smiled. She quickly moved away from the window. Lawrence passed by the bank of mailboxes in the lobby and made his way up the stairs. There were two things that his landlady found odd. He never checked his mail, and he never took the elevator.

Once in his apartment, Lawrence had two things on his mind, reset his mail account and try and get some rest before he left. As he accessed his mail account, he reflected on the fact that this was his only insurance policy. He had destroyed the originals years ago. Lawrence had a measured sense of confidence in the knowledge that the likelihood of anyone discovering his digitized version of the truth was next to impossible. Still, at that moment in time, he felt uncomfortable, and without even thinking, he inserted a disk into the floppy drive and copied the contents of his mailbox. He removed the disk and walked over to the sofa and collapsed into it.

He held the disk in front of him staring at it, wondering why he had copied it, and more importantly, what was he going to do with it. He answered his first question almost instantaneously. He had learned long ago to always follow his first instinct without asking questions. That philosophy had served him well over the years in both his personal and professional lives. The second question was a little more difficult to answer. He laid the disk on his chest and closed his eyes. He would worry about it later. He had to rest now.

Jason sat motionless at his terminal. He had been inside Lawrence's mailbox at precisely the same time and he was struck with an idea. He could not believe that he had not thought of it prior to now. He jumped from his chair and sprinted across the room to the closed door to Conner's office. He gently knocked and then began to pound on the door. An irritated Conner opened the door.

"Yes Mr. Wheeler," he said.

"Sir, I have an idea."

"I am listening," Conner said.

"I think I have found a way for us to use his mailbox to trace his location."

"Go on," Conner said.

"Have you ever heard of reverse engineering?" Jason asked.

"Refresh my memory," replied Conner.

"Reverse engineering is used to establish patent fraud. You take a finished product and work it backward to find out its origin and to find out what parts of the whole were used to create it."

"I see, and how does that help us in our present situation?" Conner asked.

"The philosophy is the same. If we can keep him on line long enough, we can trace the path back to its source."

"You mean we can actually locate where he might be holed up," Conner said.

"Yes Sir. The only problem is keeping him online for a long enough period of time to complete the trace."

"Well, what are you waiting for? Get cracking. I like the creative thinking. Get back to me once you have the logistics figured out," Conner said.

Conner returned to his office and shut the door. He seemed to recall during his last motivational speech that he had told Jason to examine that possibility. Rather than chastise his little geek, he let it pass, making Jason feel good about his contribution. He began preparing his brief for posting on the Web Page.

The brief included the steps they were taking in retracing the last known contact with the target, as well as the removal of intelligence gathering equipment from the target's home. Conner went into the scenario Jason Wheeler had approached him with in order to justify the fact that he had not taken out the source of the target's information. If the shit hit the fan, it would be Jason's idea not his.

That plan, coupled with the fact that they were still trying to locate the server that held the information, comforted him in the fact that his employer could not raise too much hell. He went on to request that his employer provide him with a detailed accounting of the target's financial affairs over the last three years. Conner wanted that information, because with it they could possibly determine a pattern or a behavior that could lead him to his quarry.

With the target's financial records, credit card purchases, bank statements showing deposits and withdrawals, and grocery store purchases, they could determine set patterns. Grocery store purchases, in particular, were made even more interesting by the tremendous databases created by the advent of the valued customer cards. The introductions of these cards were an advertiser's dream and were viewed by customers as primarily good because of the discounts available for having one.

Generally, customers did not realize the intrusion on personal privacy that they really represented. Once you filled out the little application and were issued the bar-coded cards for scanning at the checkout counter, everything you purchased went into a database under your name.

These databases were then sold to marketing firms for use in their advertising campaigns. It was not long until the government, as well as individuals like Conner, found value in such databases. Those types of databases were found everywhere. They were present in video stores, pharmacies, and service stations. Establishing a personal profile on someone had entered a new era. Personal privacy was indeed gone, and your life was an open book for anyone with the right tools.

It was 6:00pm by the time Conner finished the brief. He put on his jacket and walked out of his office and out of the warehouse without saying a word.

# Chapter - - 14

Lawrence awoke refreshed, as well as surprised. He had not expected to be able to sleep. Taking a nap was a new and unique experience for him. He walked to the bathroom and looked at his reflection in the mirror. He looked tired, and he was. He was also in a rather frisky mood. Perhaps it was the events of the last few days that had breathed life into his dull tedious life. Whatever the reason, he felt alive. He turned the faucet on and splashed his face with cold water.

He grabbed his backpack, which contained his laptop and other essentials, and was out the door. He stood in the foyer looking through the glass at the activity on the street.

He carefully looked at each car that passed and at each person to see if he noticed a familiar face. Once he was comfortable, he exited and began his round-a-bout journey to retrieve his car and supplies from Lucky's Rentown yard. Never taking the same route to any one destination, he decided to stop at a coffee shop for a large coffee and bagel.

He once again stood and looked across the street at his destination. As he sipped on his coffee, he realized how truly addicted he was to his own blend. This coffee would have to do, and it was better than the swill Lucky served.

Taking his time, he again looked at each car and each person making certain he had not been followed. Finally satisfied, he dashed across the street and into Lucky's Rentown. Lucky appeared from the front office and without exchanging a word both men made their way through the gate and into the back of the yard.

"Glad to see you could make it," Lucky said.

"Any problem getting what I requested?" asked Lawrence.

"What, are you kidding me? Piece of cake," Lucky said in a rather sarcastic tone of voice.

"What's the damage?" asked Lawrence.

"Ok, the car is gonna run ya 6 G's. Now that is my weekly rate, but seeins how you are a return customer, and seein how I like ya and all, I am gonna do the whole deal for the 4 G's. Believe me, that's a good price," he said.

Lawrence was not in the mood or in the position to dicker so he dug into his backpack and paid Lucky.

"Where are the extras?" Lawrence asked.

"In the trunk. Whatta ya think I am gonna carry the shit around or what?" Lucky replied.

Lawrence moved to the rear of the black Mercedes and opened the trunk. There, laid out nice and neat were the items he had requested.

"Are the trolling motors charged?" he asked.

"Is the Pope Catholic? Does a bear shit in the woods?" replied Lucky.

Lawrence smiled and shut the trunk. He shook hands with Lucky and got in the car. Lucky approached the driver's window.

"Seeins how we have become so close and all, you gotta name?" Lucky asked.

"Yes," he said, as he rolled up the window and drove off. He watched Lucky throw his hands up into the air in his rear view mirror.

Mike Baker was back in his office. His anger with the progress of the Dogwatch had subsided under the prospects for a brighter tomorrow with the addition of Chase Walters to the Group. Although the situation was still unsatisfactory, it had in fact become at the least tolerable. He had checked the web for updates while in his car, as well as in his office, every hour on the hour since his conversation with Conner. Finally, he found what he was looking for. An update.

As he viewed the brief prepared for him by Conner, he treated it like a schoolteacher grading a term paper. Much to his surprise, by the end of the brief, he had graded it A+ work. He liked the aggressive nature, as well as the proposed use of Lawrence's mail account, to track him. He was unhappy in regards to only one single point. They still had not been able to identify the server on which the information was stored.

Servers were scattered all over the globe, each one storing vast amounts of information. Identifying one server would prove to be a challenge, not impossible, but a challenge. Mike posted a brief statement on the Web Page congratulating Conner and the team in their progress and encouraging them to complete their assignment.

Lawrence parked the black Mercedes in the corner of the employee parking lot located across the street from the entrance to Rivermont. He produced the binoculars and proceeded to watch the guards manning the front gate. As the evening turned even darker, a light rain began to fall. He watched as the guards rotated every hour. One man remained at the gate, and one would walk the grounds. He watched this exchange for the next several hours and then proceeded to the vacant house across the lake.

Parking the car in the large driveway so that it was as hidden as possible, he proceeded through the gate and found him a spot under the branches of a large elm tree. He was somewhat protected from the rain which was now falling steadily. For the next several hours, he stood and stared through the binoculars at the hole that was to be his destination. Throughout the entire evening he had taken notes, writing down the patterns of the two guards, as well as his thoughts and ideas.

Just before dawn, he returned to the comfort of his car, started it and turned on the heat, eagerly anticipating the rush of hot air. He placed the notepad and the binoculars into his backpack and returned to the parking lot where he had begun his evening. As he watched the groundskeepers, restaurant employees, and caddies arrive, he noticed that prior to granting access to any of them, the grounds were patrolled by several men.

Lawrence assumed that this was to sweep the grounds for any possible breach overnight. They might be looking for any number of things. Some of which might include, explosives, recording devices, and any other form of threat to the privacy expected by its members.

Once the grounds were secure, the employees were granted access. They went about their duties preparing for another day of catering to the rich and famous and loathing not only their jobs, but also the people they served.

Lawrence was tired. It had been a long evening, and the coffee and other stimulants were long gone from his system. He put the car into drive and exited the parking lot. Rather than driving back to the city, he parked the car at the train station on the outskirts of town. He would catch the commuter train into the city and take a combination of busses and cabs back to the apartment. It was only a twenty-five minute train ride, and he slept for twenty-four of those minutes.

The train slowly pulled into the station. Lawrence was jostled back to reality by the screeching breaks and the mad rush of passengers all eager to be the first to exit. Lawrence continued to sit as he watched as everyone got off of the commuter train. He also watched the platform outside. Still cautious and somewhat paranoid, he finally got off and made his way to the taxi stand located outside of the station.

After two cab rides and two bus transfers, Lawrence found himself standing on the corner across the street from his apartment. Once again, he watched. He didn't wait long because he was exhausted. Once in the apartment, he tossed his backpack on the bed and collapsed on the sofa. He was asleep before his head hit the pillow.

Conner had spent the evening first in a dive that some might call a restaurant. Then he found himself wandering the streets and back alleys of the industrial neighborhood where the command center was located. He had not wanted to return to the warehouse. He needed some time to think.

Conner was used to being a man of action, and lately, he found himself being cooped up in a cramped office dispensing orders and giving direction. His had always been a life filled with excitement and adventure. Now it was comprised of decision-making and pressure. Sure he had always been responsible for other men in a command type situation, but this was different. He was not sure how it was different, but he sure felt like it was. After his head had cleared and he felt somewhat revitalized, he returned to the warehouse.

Victor and Carlos had returned to the area surrounding the office where Lawrence worked and where they had their last known contact with him. Victor was back in the Blazer, and he watched as Carlos approached. He was carrying a medium sized sports bag.

"The car is still in the garage, and the office is empty. I found this in the alley behind the office. It was by a construction dumpster they are using for renovations on one of the floors. The only item in the bag was a tie, and guess what?"

"Is it the same tie he was wearing when we lost him?" Victor said.

"Give that man a cigar. You are correct. The way I figure it, he changed, dumped the clothes down the chute, and left. He probably walked right by us. Transients got to the bag and took everything."

"Except for the tie that is," Victor said.

"Yes, except for the tie. What does a bum need with a tie?" Carlos replied.

"Good point," Victor replied.

"Alright, we need to check the security cams in the area, see if we can get a look at our man," Victor said as he produced a map.

"You take this side of the street and work your way around to here."

He said as he thumped his finger on the map, attempting to show who was in charge.

"I will take the other side of the street and work my way to there. Meet back here when you're done. Do you have your fun badge?"

"You bet, hot off the press. I have been itching to use this. Do you think I look like Secret Service?" Carlos said as he held the identification badge next to his face.

"Sure," Victor said as he laughed.

Both men exited the Blazer and headed in opposite directions with the same goal. Find the face of the man who had slipped past them.

Conner walked from the confines of his office carrying the freshly printed pages that represented the financial life and times of Lawrence Brazelton. Information was a funny thing, when looking at it as a whole it seemed somewhat useless, a mass of numbers, places and digits that seemed to stretch for an eternity.

The key was to assemble the information into smaller more manageable chunks. That is where Jason Wheeler came into play. He would take the information contained on those pages and on the disk he had copied and translate it into more meaningful terms. The power of the computer coupled with a mind such as his could easily dissect the information and then reassemble it into usable data.

"Wheeler, I need you to filter this information and come up with some patterns. I need to know where this man shopped, where he ate, what he liked, and when he liked it. You know the drill." Conner said.

"Yes Sir," Jason replied as he reached for the stack of information.

Jason Wheeler was a geek, and that was a rather simple deduction. He looked the part and acted it as well. He lived for this type of thing. When he worked on these types of projects, he was in his element. He eagerly accepted the task.

"And Wheeler, I need it yesterday," Conner said.

Jason simply smiled, and Conner took the smile as both acceptance and understanding. He knew what this type of assignment meant for Jason, and he knew that the boy would not let him down.

"And one other thing, I need for you to run down a scenario on the possibility of our tapping into the NSA computer system. I understand that they are developing a program for monitoring all of the video produced in the city. You know, security cams in stores, ATM's and traffic cams etc."

"I heard about that," Jason replied.

"No doubt from your conspiracy minded friends on the Internet," Conner replied.

"Yeah, I heard that if the beta test in D.C. goes well, they are going to wire up the country. I guess my so called "conspiracy buddies" were right."

"Need I remind you, our work is not the topic for conversation during your little chat sessions online?" Conner said.

"I know, and not to worry, I mainly listen. You know I get a lot of useful information from those crackpots. They have been on the mark on more than one occasion."

"Too bad no one ever takes them seriously," Conner said.

"No doubt, they have nailed a few of our Ops in the past. Not that they knew who we were or anything, but they nailed the purpose."

"I know, I have read the crap they post. I know you like to think I don't pay attention to that kind of thing, but I do. To be honest, at times I have thought some of these idiots were getting too close to the truth, and if I didn't know better, I would think they were getting information from the inside," Conner said.

"I never…"

"I know. You would be dead if that were the case…." Conner said as he cut Jason off mid sentence.

"As would any member of my team who decided to talk out of school. Now get to work, and do some good."

Conner turned and walked to his office. He could smell the fear in the air, as well as the stare of Jason Wheeler. He had wanted to put a little scare into Jason and this had proven to be an excellent opportunity. Jason was a geek, not a soldier. He didn't share the same characteristics as the other men.

Conner would have rather had a real soldier as opposed to Jason. But Jason had his value, and he was good at what he did, so Conner kept him around. Every once in a while, he had to assist him in recognizing the reality and gravity of their work and that was what he had just done. There was no greater motivator than the threat of death.

Chase had not slept well at all the previous night. He was conflicted and torn by what was right and what was wrong. The reality of yesterday's encounter had left him feeling empty and violated. He had sold out his principles for money, power, and the security of secrets remaining buried. He sat in his office and contemplated his decision. He had given up his freedom, the freedom to personally make decisions, to answer only to himself and his conscience.

For that freedom he had been granted absolution for past mistakes, the opportunity to continue doing what he loved, and the financial security that would ensure his family a very comfortable life. The conflict occurred because he had not yet decided whether or not the trade was equitable. Everything had happened so fast. He was forced to make a decision right then and there, or he had at least felt that way.

As was the case with most people in compromising positions, he began to rationalize the decision he had made. Rather than looking at freedom lost, he began to look at freedom gained. Money and power bring to the table a certain freedom of their own, he thought. The thought of continued employment with the next administration brought with it additional promise. He began to feel like maybe his decision might prove to be lucrative.

What he didn't realize was that he was following the path that Mike Baker and all the men like him knew he would. Self-preservation, coupled with the influence of money and perceived power, can make a man rationalize away even the worst decisions in life. That is exactly what Chase Walters was doing. He had been manipulated by a master and was now walking down the path of ultimate self-destruction of his own free will.

Surprisingly, once again Lawrence had slept relatively well. He sat up feeling refreshed and moved across the room to his desk. He opened his notebook and began to go over the notes he had taken the previous night. He had noticed just enough patterns to make him feel comfortable about making the trip, and tonight was the night. Most of the activity occurred during the dawn hours in preparation for the day. The nights were fairly calm and uneventful.

The guards rotated hourly on their patrol of the grounds and their patterns were the same with each rotation. He had calculated the time between seeing the guards at his destination and had determined that he had between 55 and 65 minutes. The guards chosen route would allow him to motor across the lake and wait just off the shore until he had passed. Once the guard had passed, he would have ample time to locate what Clay Danvers had indicated on the photograph.

His plan was coming together and the anticipation of the hunt caused the blood to course through his veins. He felt alive. He felt like he had a purpose, and he could not sit still. After he had showered and shaved, he dressed and grabbed his backpack. He was going to visit the White House, not as a guest, but as a tourist. He wanted to stand and look at the home of the man who had sent his life into a tumultuous spin of grief and loss. He wanted to stand in defiance of the man who had not only destroyed his life, but the lives of so many others.

Lawrence knew that it was not only the President who had ruined so much for so many. He knew that there were others. However, just like looking into the eyes of a murderer in court, it is not the body of the man you remember, it is the head, the face, the eyes of the man. Cut off the head and the body dies, he thought. He hoped that that were true, because he was about to test that theory.

# Chapter - - 15

Today was the day that the President was to bury a friend, to put to rest a man whose life had ended too soon. Preston Wesley was a man who, on the outside, appeared to have it all together. He was a man who exuded confidence and conviction. He embodied the inner strength that most people envied. Inside, he was a man in conflict.

He was troubled by his past and in need of someone to reassure him. Clay Danvers had been that person. Since his death, the President had been wrestling with the decisions he had made in his life.

Chase Walters had noticed it, and now he had to be the man to replace Danvers. His understanding of the situation, as well as the relationship, had been clarified. He had often wondered why the President had relied so heavily on the advice of Danvers and why there had been so many private meetings between the two. He finally had the answers.

The President was a puppet, a front man, who could not act or move unless his strings were manipulated. He had no will to act on his own, no ability. Chase had known all along that this type of thing went on in Washington. But like so many others, he had denied that it could go on so close to him. Besides, he liked to take the credit in those situations.

Denial was a way of life in the Capital. It was the lifeblood that made it possible to cope with the life that was politics. His coping skills had just been dealt a blow. He had a new reality, but he was warming up to it. He found himself in the role of the puppet master, and if he were honest, he would have to say the idea was beginning to appeal to him. For as long as he could remember he had been labeled the man behind the President's decisions. He didn't mind the label and did little to dispel the myth. Now that myth was quickly turning into reality.

His smile grew even wider as he approached the door to the President's private residence. He gently knocked and turned to look at the two secret service agents that were always posted outside the door.

"He is expecting you.  You can go on in," one of the agents said.

Without a word and with only a simple nod of his head, he opened the door.  Sitting in a chair with his head in his hands was the President.

"Mr. President?" he said.

"Mr. President?" he repeated.

Slowly, the President raised his head.  The emotion was evident in his face.  He looked as though he had aged ten years since the last time Chase had seen him.  His eyes were bloodshot, and he had those familiar bags underneath them.  The corners of his mouth were turned down, and the wrinkles that accompany a frown were abundantly evident around his mouth, as well as plastered across his forehead.

The President looked weak, and he looked defeated.  Chase knew that this could prove to be bad, and at the same time, if it were handled properly, he could be the photo- op that continued to define an administration.  It was time to manipulate the strings and make his puppet spring to life.  Chase pulled a chair up next to the President and began to work the strings.


Lawrence had made his way to the front of the White House.  Pennsylvania Avenue had been closed to traffic sometime ago.  Despite that fact, it had remained open to pedestrian traffic.  He watched as several tourists stood in front of the massive fence that surrounded the White House and posed for pictures.  Across the street, he noted that all the anti-Government groups were demonstrating as usual.  As he panned the area, he noted an unusually large contingent of police, secret service, and other security forces.

Then it hit him.  Today was the day, the day that Clay Danvers was to be put to rest.  The President, as well as just about every other member of the White House, would be attending the funeral.

Feeling a little less confident of his decision to visit the White House, he quickly blended in with a group of tourists as they made their way back to a tour bus.  He had realized that with POTUS (**P**resident **o**f **t**he **U**nited **S**tates), leaving the

118

grounds, as well as the vast majority of other officials, security would be tight. The secret service would be photographing and filming the crowds that had assembled. It was common practice for the secret service to do such things on a day such as this, when it is publicly known the President would be out.

Once the intelligence is gathered, agents process it and then cross check each individual in the crowd with other crowds from previous outings. If an individual is noted more than once, they are put into a database and cataloged as a possible threat. Lawrence was a threat. He didn't know if they were aware of it yet, but he was a threat. Feeling somewhat sheepish and uneasy, he quickly and quietly made his way out of the crowd and out of the area.


The President was feeling better. Life had returned to his face, and his confidence was now beginning to resurface. Chase reached out and took the speech back from the President.

"That is a wonderful piece of writing Chase," the President said.

"You have talented people around you Sir, all working to see to your best interests."

"Indeed I do. Indeed I do," replied the President.

"Mr. President?"

"Yes Chase?"

"Sir, I know that the death of Mr. Danvers has come as a great shock to you. I know how close you were, and I know how much you relied on his counsel. I want you to know that I feel as though when one door closes, another one is opened."

"I am not sure I am following you," replied the President.

"What I am trying to say is that I am on your team Sir. We have known each other for a long time, and we have worked together much of that time. I think I know you as well as anybody. I have your interests at heart. I am concerned about continuing to build your legacy and assuring your place in history."

"Go on," the President said.

"I don't want you to look at this as a loss Sir. I want you to look at it as an opportunity. You have done so much for your country. Unemployment is at an all time low. We have experienced a budget surplus that is unsurpassed by any other administration. Americans are happy."

Chase let his compliments hang in the air without saying another word. Having been briefed on the relationship between the President and Clay Danvers, he knew exactly where he was going. The puppet master watched as the life and energy began to flow in the room. He found it rather ironic that the most powerful man in the free world was just as nervous and insecure as the majority of the general public.

"An opportunity. I like that," the President said.

"Yes, an opportunity. An opportunity to seize today and see that the day does not end here, an opportunity for you to continue to build upon your great works, as well as ensure that those efforts continue on into the new century," Chase replied.

Chase was pulling on the right strings. He was focusing not on the misdeeds of the past, but on the promise of a better tomorrow. The balance between the President and his allies was delicate, and Chase Walters had begun his mastery of that delicate balancing act.

The President knew of the existence of the Group. He knew that they were there, operating in the shadows and manipulating the system. He chose not to acknowledge their presence. It was a deal struck long ago in a different time and place. Like Chase Walters, he had gone through the moral dilemma of giving up his freedom, and he had also rationalized away the guilt. The Group had always kept him out of the loop. Somehow the arrangement had worked just fine.

The President had known that Clay Danvers was the conduit through which the Group had operated. He had felt almost a peace upon hearing of his death. He thought that the ties to the Group might have been severed. With his administration coming to a close after two terms in office, he felt like maybe he was free at last. But that feeling was slowly leaving the room as he sat and talked with Chase. The President was not ignorant.

He was a well-traveled man, once a top-notch lawyer. He was the consummate politician who had been blessed with the ability to connect with people, to read them, and understand them. He now knew that the Group had quickly filled the position left vacant by Clay Danvers. He was alone and having a conversation with his replacement right now. The nightmare would continue. The link between a President and a band of self-serving capitalists had not been broken, as he had hoped. It had just been reengineered.

The funeral was attended by a virtual "who's who" of the political world. Clay Danvers neighbor had come to pay her respects. Her son stood silently by her side holding a leash. They had brought Clay's dog, Springer, out of respect. They thought he might have appreciated the gesture. They stood outside the old century style church and watched as invited guests arrived and entered.

The President's speech was received well, and by all accounts, it would increase his favorable ratings in the overnight polls. He connected on a personal front, as well as a political front. He came off as caring, kind, and compassionate, as well as forceful, committed, and ready to seize the future.

Chase Walters sat in awe as the President hit his mark on practically every point. The tears flowed at precisely the right moment. The dedication and assertiveness appeared on cue. He knew the President was a master at delivering a knock out speech, and today was no exception.

As they made their way from the church to the limousine for the procession back to the White House, the President was seen to be smiling at times and then tearing up full of emotion. Chase watched the Jekyll and Hyde transformations and noted that they occurred on cue and only when the President was in view of the press. He had seen it so many times, and yet, it still amazed him.

They sat silently in the limousine for what seemed to be an eternity when Chase turned to speak and break the uncomfortable silence. As both men's eyes met in the backseat of the presidential limousine, Chase realized that no words needed to be exchanged. He knew at that precise moment that both men were now officially on the same page. Both men realized their particular role and words would never have to be exchanged regarding it.

Chase turned and looked out the window. Feeling somewhat uneasy, he wondered, who was the puppet, and who was the puppet master.

Conner had watched the funeral and the speech given by the President. He was less than moved by the whole event. He knew the real man, the man behind the mask, but watched anyway. The rest of the team had returned from their assigned duties in the field, and he rose from his chair and headed for the conference table in the main part of the warehouse.

"Ladies, let's get started. Nathan, lets have it."

"I retrieved all of our equipment from the target's house. Jason has the keyboard bug and is going over the information again. I also took the liberty of lifting a set of his prints."

"A set of prints? Why?" Asked Conner.

"Ah, you never know if we might need them for planting later. You know what they say about DNA and fingerprints."

"Save it Nathan," Conner said.

"Mr. Wheeler?" Conner continued.

"Nothing so far. We pretty much have everything already."

"Please continue," Conner said.

"That's pretty much it. Oh yeah, his lady was still there, and I had to wait. So I took the liberty of tagging her car," Nathan said.

"A, for effort and ingenuity my boy. Victor, Carlos, did you bring anything to the party?" Conner asked.

"Sir, we retrieved several security tapes from locations surrounding the target's office. We pulled only the tapes from the time we last spotted the target to the time we entered his office to verify his absence," Victor said.

"Very good, and what have you brought to the party Carlos?" Conner said.

"We found several transients wearing different items of clothing belonging to the target. Best scenario we can come up with is that he got spooked and bolted. We found a sports bag with his tie in it by a construction dumpster they are using for renovations on one of the floors in the building. He changed, dumped the clothes, and skipped," Carlos replied.

"A tie?" Conner said.

"Yes Sir, a tie. I guess bums aren't too concerned about a complete ensemble," replied Carlos.

"Very cute Carlos. Don't give up your day job," Conner said.

"Ok, it is safe to assume the target is aware that he is being sought, or he is simply spooked. He is in the open and is now considered to be a threat. We will be spending some time here. Nathan, since you were so bold as to tag his girlfriends car, it is now your assignment to monitor her movements."

"Yes Sir," Nathan replied.

"Carlos the comedian will be with me. Victor you're with Wheeler. I want you two to go over the security tapes, and get me a picture of this guy in his new digs. Okay people, let's get on it. Wheeler, can I see you?"

As the others moved off in their own direction to pursue their new assignments, Jason followed Conner towards his office.

"Yes Sir," replied Jason.

"Did you obtain the information I requested?"

"Yes Sir."

He handed Conner a folder with the words "No Secrets" written in bold red marker on the front.

"Very good young man. We may have to keep you around for another day," Conner said.

"Now get the hell outta here and impress me some more will ya."

"Yes Sir," replied Jason.

As Jason turned to leave, Carlos approached the office. Once again the hunt was on, and it was only a matter of time.

Lawrence had made his way safely back to the coffee shop across the street from his apartment. It was the only place that served his brand of coffee, but that was the last thing on his mind right now. He sat in a booth at the rear of the establishment and ordered a large coffee and a bagel. He spent several minutes calling into question his sanity for even going near the White House of all places, especially today.

"Stupid… Stupid… Stupid…" Lawrence said in a low voice.

"Excuse me?" replied a very confused waitress standing next to the table.

Lawrence looked up and saw the waitress had returned and was standing at the side of the booth holding his coffee and bagel.

"Sorry, it's nothing. I am just talking to myself," he said.

"Pretty harsh words. Hope you weren't talking about me," she said.

"No, it's just been one of those days, and it's still pretty much morning," replied Lawrence.

"Well, if I can get you anything else darling, you just holler," she said.

"Thanks, I will," he replied.

What else can go wrong, he wondered? He also wondered if they had snapped a photograph of him during his little excursion. Would it really matter, he thought? After all, there was no other photograph of him to cross check it against. He wasn't on any threat board, or was he? Now he was worried. If ever anyone were considered a threat, it would be him. But would the President have enlisted the secret service?

Lawrence had to regain his composure, and he had to relax. He stirred in some crème and sugar into his coffee, and as he began to sip it, he heard a familiar voice. He re-positioned himself in his booth so he could see the television over the counter. Preston Wesley was in the middle of his speech.

He sat and listened to the man talk about this great nation, its tremendous prosperity, and the unselfish service of great men like Clay Danvers. As the President continued, Lawrence blocked out the sound in his head and concentrated on only the face and the mannerisms of the President. His hatred and disdain for the man grew with each gesture, each time he bit his lip and furled his brow. Lawrence hated the man who had everything and who had taken away everything he had.

"Could someone turn the channel?" he blurted out.

He turned and concentrated on his coffee and bagel. At least he had his coffee. He was grateful for finding an establishment that served his special blend. He began to go over the events that would transpire that evening.

Conner sat and read the material that Jason had gathered. It focused on the intelligence community's beta test of gathering information via pirated signals from targeted video sources. It was appropriately code named "No Secrets." The public in general never took the conspiracy buffs seriously, and they were considered nuts, pure and simple. The truth of the matter was that they were more often closer to the mark than they were nuts.

He had first learned about its existence through his employer, who at the time thought this type of technology would come in handy in the future. As Conner continued to read the information, he soon realized the true scope and grandeur of this venture. If this program ever saw the light of day, it would seriously disrupt the very definition of personal privacy.

A series of satellites would be placed in orbit. These satellites numbered two at present and were focused solely on cities in the United States. All video transmissions are digitized and relayed from one point to another. This is done via transmitters for over-the-air broadcast, cable for point-to-point broadcast, etc. This technology made it possible to pin point a transmission source via a satellite. Once the signal had been intercepted, it was then sent to a central monitoring station. The technique was called, Signal cloning. All of this was being done without the knowledge of either the sender or the receiver.

As an example, you could literally see what was occurring at the local mini mart by simply intercepting the signal as it was taken from a security camera and transmitted to the unit recording it. Conner set the information down, put his head in his hands and began to laugh out loud.

# Chapter - - 16

Lawrence was busy pacing his apartment floor still concerned about his venture out earlier that day. Several hours had passed since his return, yet he still felt like an idiot for making the decision to go in the first place. As he regained his focus, he turned to his desk and grabbed his laptop, taking time to make sure he gathered everything he needed and packed it properly. Once he had gathered up his wares, he headed for the door.

Opening the door, he stopped suddenly in his tracks snapping his fingers. He walked over to the modest bookshelf that adorned the wall adjacent to the window and removed a book. Opening the book, he removed the diskette that contained the downloaded version of his information.

"Don't leave home without it!" he exclaimed as he kissed the disk.

With that, he was out the door. He could not just sit around that small apartment and do nothing. As he made his way down the stairs and to the lobby, the door to his landlady's apartment flew open just as he had passed it. It startled Lawrence, which in turn startled her.

"You got a package today. Wait here and I'll get it," she said.

Lawrence watched as she turned and went back inside. He was struck with sudden fear. It was the kind of fear that is paralyzing. The heart stops, you can't breathe, and you can't move. His mind went wild. Who would know to send me anything? Who knows I am here? He wanted to run, but he couldn't. A curious mix of fear and curiosity held him in place. He watched the door, waiting for her to return. He heard the sound of those ugly slippers as they tapped and then slid on the wood floor. The sound became louder as she came closer.

"Here. They sent one to everyone in the building," she said as she handed the package to him.

"Some kind of promotion I think," she continued.

Lawrence stood there for a moment longer still reeling from the shock. Finally, it registered in his mind, his body began to relax, and he regained the ability to both move and speak.

"Why didn't you just put it in my box?" he said.

"Cause you never check your box," she snapped back.

"And how may I ask, do you know I don't check my box?" he inquired.

"You live here long enough, you know these things," she replied as she turned and walked back to her door slamming it behind her.

Lawrence stood there holding the box for several seconds before even looking at it. As he glanced down, he saw that the package that had put the fear of God in him was merely a box of detergent with an attached survey form.

"A promotional survey," he muttered.

After going through his routine at the lobby entrance of checking the street, he exited the building, and tossed the package in the first trash container he came to. Lawrence turned at the corner and headed north. He was going to the movies. It was the perfect place to be and not be seen.

Mike Baker sat in his office and finally turned the television off. He had watched practically every news program for the reaction to the day's events. By all accounts the President had come out a winner. Political popularity was a most curious phenomenon.

No matter how skilled you might be, no matter how brilliant your decisions and policies were, if you could not connect with people, you were doomed. Preston Wesley could connect, and people responded. He had a charisma, a charm about him. He could make you feel as though you mattered, and the people responded.

One thing, in particular, that Mike looked for was the presence of his new acquisition, Chase Walters. Mike studied his demeanor and his mannerisms very carefully during the many different news outtakes. By virtue of the performance given by the President, as well as the way in which Walters had appeared, Mike knew that things were going to work out just fine. Taking into consideration the report by Clay Danvers during their last meeting, the Group had developed some concerns over the President's commitment and resilience. Today's events and the performance by the President helped to alleviate some of those concerns.

Going over the videotapes retrieved by Carlos and Victor was a slow process. Jason had decided that the process would go faster if they divided the tapes. He set up a television and VCR for Victor. Both men sat with their eyes glued to the screens.

"How will we know if it's him when we see him?" asked Victor.

"You probably won't. Just look for anyone who matches the general physical characteristics, then freeze frame, and copy it over to the computer like I showed you. Once we have been through them all, we can start to tweak the pictures and see if we can find our man," Jason said.

"Just because we find him on the tapes, how's that gonna help us find him? Man this sucks!" Victor said.

"Listen, first of all if we find him, we will know what looks like now. If we know how he is dressed, we can guess where he might go," replied Jason.

"And exactly how is that?" asked Victor.

"Simple, you don't dress up if your going underground, and you don't dress down if your going up town. Secondly, we can establish which direction he might be headed. Last, and most important, if we can get a picture of this guy in his present state, it will give us something to cross check for reference against future photographs and locations."

"What future photographs, and what future locations?" asked Victor.

"Just a little project we are looking into. Listen, don't worry about it, and just get to finding the guy, will ya?"

"Yeah, yeah, I hear ya," replied Victor.

Jason continued to view the screen scanning for any person who fit the general physical description. He turned and looked at Victor and then turned his attention back to his monitor. He knew if he tried to explain to him the details of what they were doing and purpose for it, he would not understand. Victor was a warrior, a soldier, and he was only interested in destroying things.

Jason had never held a weapon, never destroyed anything. Well, not in the sense that the other members of the team had. Yes, he was different, but that was ok. He liked what he did, and he enjoyed the perks of his employer. He had state of the art technology at his fingertips and the license to do pretty much anything with it.

In the outside world, in the real world, he would be arrested and prosecuted for the things he did. Most of his friends had either ended up in jail for hacking, on the run, or working for some large corporation selling out the trade. None of these options suited Jason. He had found a home and a venue for his talents.

It had started out as a warm fall day but was quickly turning into a damp and dreary one. Lawrence had spent the early portion of the afternoon engaged in a series of cat and mouse type activities. He was not sure whether he was the cat or the mouse. His first activity was a movie, then a local street market.

He maneuvered through the crowd of people with his head down and making eye contact with no one. He could not shake the feeling of stupidity from his morning venture to the White House. The afternoon sun had long since disappeared behind a series of clouds that threatened rain.

As he walked through the street market, it indeed began to rain. First, just a drop here and there, then a more steady rainfall ensued. Lawrence raised his head and watched as the local vendors began to scurry about. First attempting to cover their wares, then trying to seek shelter for themselves. Some returned to their shops others scampered for their vehicles.

Under normal circumstances, walking in the rain would have been completely unacceptable to him. The expensive suits and shoes and coifed hair would cause him to react much like the people he was watching. The new Lawrence, this Lawrence, was actually enjoying the experience. It brought out a freedom he had long since forgotten.

As he continued to walk, he kicked at the puddles now forming both in the street, as well as on the sidewalks. He looked towards the sky, allowing the rain to fall on his face. Lawrence opened his mouth and let the raindrops tickle the end of his tongue. This had been just what he had needed. He checked his watch and decided it was time to make his way back to his rented car for the drive to Rivermont.

Tonight was the night, and the rain was going to make his job much easier. He flipped up the collar of his jacket, pulled his cap tighter on his head, and hailed a taxi at the corner.

Kelly Ford had not followed the admonition of Lawrence. Instead, she had returned to her house and had spent the past several days waiting. Her computer had remained on and she checked her E-mail on a regular basis. She carried her pager around with her from room to room. Standing a little less than 6', she was a strikingly beautiful woman, brown hair, brown eyes, and a tremendously fit athletic build. She had an above average IQ, and during her college, years the intelligence community heavily recruited her.

Her father was in the Air Force, and Kelly traveled during much of her youth. She was fluent in several languages and was familiar with life abroad. All of these characteristics made her an ideal candidate for intelligence work. She had spent the past several days reflecting on her life and her decisions. She was now in conflict with some aspects of her life and some of the decisions she had made. It was not the waiting that was difficult. It was the pain of a life that was torn in conflict.

Across town, Paul Justin sat in an office he had now begun to call home. He had just dismissed his staff, which included several lawyers, FBI investigators assigned to him, and an assortment of other staffers. It was late and the meeting had gone well, all things considered. He was now going over news clippings that were provided to him by a local agency.

This agency read every newspaper published and clipped any and all articles relating to a particular client. In this case, the client happened to be Paul Justin. Any mention of the

Independent Counsel was clipped and added to a daily portfolio that he would then read. The majority of articles were less than flattering. The investigation into the President had traveled down many roads that were mired in innuendo and confusion. There was no clear-cut evidence that could lead to the prosecution of the President, no smoking gun. As he read the daily clippings, he wondered if it was worth the effort and the daily vilification.

The President of the United States was a popular man. The economy was robust, unemployment was at an all time low, and the country was indeed prospering. The result was a public that had been manipulated to embrace a corrupt man, based solely on the fact that as long as John Q public had his, he did not care about the deeds of the man that was perceived to have given it to him. As a result, the Independent Counsel was viewed as a bully, and Paul Justin was viewed as a man with a grudge and a personal agenda.

The truth in fact was far from a simple grudge. Prior to serving as Independent Counsel, Paul Justin had been a respected lawyer, as well as a judge. During his legal life, which now represented the majority of his existence on this earth, he had been a witness to many things, some good and some bad.

He loved the law, he loved his country, and he believed in both. When he was appointed to the office, both parties had viewed him as the best man for the job. Although the honeymoon was short lived, he pursued his role with the same drive and integrity that had earned him the respect of his peers. With blinders on, he pushed for the truth. Taking on a President, a popular President, was not an easy task. In an era where the media shapes public opinion and public opinion shapes political ideologies and direction, he found he was fighting a losing battle. The old axiom, "You can't fight City Hall," rang in his ears.

The country loved prosperity, and the country loved Preston Wesley. Given even a shadow of doubt, they would stand behind him. No other President had experienced this level of public apathy, and no other President had escaped the scrutiny of the press and public like Preston A. Wesley.

Perhaps that was Paul Justin's motivation. Perhaps he was bitter for not being able to do to his President what so many other special prosecutors had done to theirs. His frustration level was at an all time high. Every time he was almost able to grab the brass ring, it was yanked out of his reach. He had not heard from Lawrence Brazelton in some time and with the death of Clay Danvers coming so close to his meeting with Lawrence, he knew he was close to something. His years on both sides of the bench had sharpened his senses. There was blood in the water and he could smell it.

Lawrence was sitting in his rented car at the "park and ride" where he had left it. He watched as the commuters came and went, carrying their brief cases, purses, and newspapers, using them as makeshift umbrellas. He watched as the rain hit his windshield, and he held mini impromptu races between the drops of rain that raced down the glass. He watched as the parking lot slowly emptied. It reminded him of watching ants' parade in a straight line out of an anthill as a child. As the sun set behind the thick blanket of clouds in the western sky, Lawrence started his car and joined the parade.

The drive at first was slow. He was traveling in the same direction as many of the commuters. As he came closer to his destination, the traffic began to thin out, and the drive became a little more tolerable. As he exited the freeway he decided to check out the entrance and the employee parking lot before heading to the house across the lake. The scene was exactly as he had anticipated. The rain had done its job.

The Country Club was empty and only the two guards remained. Not wanting to draw any unnecessary attention to himself, he continued to drive without stopping. As he made the drive to the vacant house, he could feel the nervous tension building in his stomach. He tried to remember when he had felt such nervous energy. Was it the first time he rose in a court of law and faced a jury? Was it when he first realized that he had to live the rest of his life without his wife and his son? He couldn't ever remember a time when he had felt like this.

He drove past the house once to make sure that it was still empty. It was. He circled the block, pulled into the circular driveway, and then backed the Mercedes sedan around to the side of the house.

He sat in the car for what seemed like an eternity, gripping the wheel until his knuckles turned first red, then ash white. He resorted to giving himself a pep talk like he did before his final summations as an attorney. As his heart slowed and his breathing became relaxed, he released his grip on the steering wheel and exited the car.

He moved to the trunk and removed the supplies Lucky had procured for him. The rain was still falling at a pretty good pace. He made his way to the dock and emptied his belongings into the bow of the smaller boat. Sitting on the back of the small launch, he attached the small electric motor.

He had asked for two motors in the event of any unforeseen complications. He checked his watch. It was 10:30. He reached for the switch to turn on the small engine and realized he had forgotten something. He made his was back to the car, and just as he was opening the trunk, he noticed what he thought was a light. It was growing brighter and coming closer to the car. He ducked down behind the car on the passenger side and watched as the light danced around the massive lawn of the house and traced the circular driveway. As the light grew even brighter and closer, Lawrence felt his heart pounding in his chest.

Just as Lawrence had feared he would be discovered, the light went out. He slowly moved from behind the car and watched as the rent a cop pulled away. He had not even considered a neighborhood watch. He waited a moment and attempted to regain his composure. As his heart rate and breathing began to return to a somewhat normal pace, he opened the trunk and reached inside.

He produced the gun that he had instructed Lucky to obtain. He was afraid of guns. He hated them, but his fear had led him to own one now. He tucked the gun into his waistband and made his way down the path to the dock. He sat in the small launch and started the electric motor. It was surprisingly quiet, and the rain muffled any noise that was evident as it hit the water.

134

The small electric trolling motor was painfully slow. It took him just about 30 minutes to cross the lake. He turned off the motor and drifted to about 20 yards off the shore. Again, he checked his watch. He feared that the delay caused by his forgetfulness and the rent-a-cop might have caused him to miss the security guard as he made his rounds. The rain was falling at a much harder pace, and Lawrence watched as it pooled in the bottom of the small boat.

"That is just great. This is just what I need. I am going to sink," he muttered.

As he looked up, he saw the security guard as he made his way past Lawrence's destination and towards the lake. Flashlight in hand, the security guard half-heartedly checked his surroundings, even shinning the light into the lake. The light did not come close to where Lawrence had positioned himself. Lawrence watched as the guard followed the same path that he had witnessed earlier. As the guard and his flashlight disappeared, Lawrence again started the electric motor and continued onto shore.

Pulling the small craft ashore, Lawrence grabbed his light and the backpack and headed for the small structure where he hoped to find what Clay had left behind. There stood the small building with a green metal roof and log siding to match the Country Clubs Mountain motif. It was not much to look at. After all, it was only a bathroom. Lawrence removed the photograph that he had enclosed in a sheet protector. He looked at his watch. He figured he had 45 minutes to locate whatever it was he was meant to find.

He looked at the picture, then at the structure. He moved towards the small building and began to look around the area that was marked on the photo. He began feeling around in the wet grass at the corner. He found what appeared to be a drainage cover. Quickly and with great anticipation, he removed the lid and looked inside, and again found nothing. He picked up the lid and looked on the underside, once again, nothing.

At first he felt angry, then his anger turned to realism. He knew it couldn't be that easy. He continued his search around the area. Comfortable with the fact that he had covered the outside, he decided to move to the inside.

The door was locked, so he used the small military spade to pry the door open. Once inside and now safe from the constant rain, he removed his hat and black poncho. The inside corner was just that, a corner. He stood and stared at it for a moment, and then said out loud as he shrugged his shoulders,

"What the hell!"

He took the point of the shovel and began to break away the drywall that covered the inside corner. After he had removed large enough pieces, he reached inside the wall expecting to find something, but instead found nothing but fiberglass insulation and sawdust. Disgusted, he sat down and put his head in his hands. He reached for the photo and began to stare at it again.

"What are you trying to tell me?"

"What am I looking for?"

He looked at the mess he had made of the inside of the bathroom and decided that whatever it was, it was not in here. He stood up and put his rain poncho and hat back on and went outside. Looking at his watch, he realized he had only about 5 minutes worth of time left. The guard would not be back around for maybe 15 minutes, but he had to get back to the boat and get a comfortable distance from shore before he returned.

He moved back to the corner where he had originally started and began again to try and find anything. The search came up empty. The only thing he had not noticed the first time was a small brass plaque with the picture of a log cabin and the name of the company that had built the rather stylish log bathroom.

He was just about to display his anger at the thought of embarking on this wild goose chase when he heard, through the gentle patter of the rain on the metal roof, the bark of a dog. As he looked in the direction of the noise, he saw the flashlight of what he suspected to be the security guard. But he had a dog? He didn't remember ever seeing any dogs. He quickly began to gather his belongings and made a mad dash for the boat. He pushed it into the water, not caring that by the time he had gotten in, he was up to his thighs in water. He switched on the motor and made his way back towards the house.

He anxiously continued to check behind him and was concerned that the guard seemed to be moving at a rapid pace, attempting to keep up with the dog. He had no time left, so he cut the motor just as the dog hit the shore and barked at the black lake in the direction of Lawrence. He got on his stomach in the boat and looked over the back. The guard was standing on the shore, with the dog barking in front of him, as he traced his light back and forth across the blackness of the lake.

His heart was racing, but his fear of being discovered began to subside as the guard turned his attention back to the grounds. He could hear the man yelling at the dog as he made his way back towards the course. Lawrence rolled over onto his back and breathed a heavy sigh of relief as the rain hit his face. His relief didn't last long as he realized that the guard was sure to find the mess he had left behind. Then the guard might take the dog's barking a little more seriously.

He hit the switch on the motor and nothing happened. Panic again set in. He was sure to be caught now. Then he remembered that he had two motors, so he quickly made the change, dumping the first motor into the lake. He felt a bit more relaxed as the small craft began to make its way slowly back to the safety of the opposite shore. As he looked towards his destination, the excitement began to wane and the frustration returned. He had found nothing.

# Chapter - - 17

The Dogwatch had been following up on any leads that might bring them closer to the new identity and possible whereabouts of Lawrence Brazelton. Conner was growing steadily impatient, because the going was slow and less than productive. He had received several requests for an update from his employer. Mike Baker was particularly interested in the termination of the information suspended precariously in Lawrence's mail account.

The idea of tracing him through his Internet connection had not been productive. The only positive outcome was that they had located the server that stored the incriminating documents. Lawrence never stayed on line long enough to establish a trace, and even if he had, he was covering his tracks in a big way. Jason had thought he was close on one occasion, only to discover that the trace was a wild goose chase, a pop in Australia that led to a Unix box at MIT, and as best they could count at least a half dozen routers after that. Conner was frustrated and Jason was impressed.

Conner paced within the confines of his small office and contemplated his next move. It was obvious that they were not going to be able to smoke him out using his Internet account, and the information was a threat as long as it remained in limbo just waiting to be sent. On the other hand, if they were to take out the account, it might alert Lawrence as to the fact that someone was on to him. And the possibility still existed that there were hard copies of all the documentation somewhere.

Conner knew from past experience that it was not wise to take away all of your enemies options. It only leads to unpredictable behavior. When a man is backed into a corner, he only has two options, surrender or fight. He stopped cold in his tracks and moved towards the door. Throwing it open, he yelled,

"Wheeler!"

"Yes Sir," Jason replied in a stunned and surprised tone of voice.

"Take it down."

"But Sir, I thought…"

"I don't care what you think. You aren't paid to think unless I say so, and I am not asking you to think. I am telling you to do it!" replied Conner.

The process for taking out the server that housed the information was a simple enough task. Their employer had provided them with a copy of a worm virus. Once it was introduced into the server, it would slowly and methodically erase any and all information stored therein. Since their employer was the man behind the computer revolution, he had access to some of the most brilliant and destructive minds within the computing industry. Conner watched as Jason loaded the CD that contained the code for the virus. All eyes in the room were now focused on the actions of Jason Wheeler.

Silence fell across the large empty warehouse, and the only audible sounds were those of Jason's fingers as they danced across his keyboard. Then came the familiar sound of a dial tone and then the mystical language that computers shared to communicate. Jason sent the virus to Lawrence. Moments later, he accessed his mail account. Opening the attachment containing the virus started the chain of events that would wipe out vast amounts of information in many servers, as well as computers.

The CD began to slow down. It was apparent that the process was complete. The worm was now actively working its way through the server via Lawrence's account.

"Man this is beautiful!" he exclaimed.

"Where did you get this? It's a freaking work of art!" he continued.

"Is it done?" Conner said.

"Yea man. It's done all right, and there is going to be some pissed off people. This thing is nasty. I bet we make the evening news with this," replied Jason.

"Good. Now we can all get back to work. I want this man found. He may or may not know that someone is on to him. He might think some hacker out for kicks erased his program, as well as everyone else's. Then again, he might just prove to be as smart as I think he is. In which case, I suggest someone bring me something I can use. Now move it!" Conner said as he turned and headed for his office.

As Mike Baker sat in the safety and comfort of his office, a quiet chaos erupted. In households and businesses all across the country, people were surfing the Internet, reading and sending E-mail. Slowly systems began to crash, screens displayed meaningless jargon, and eventually faded to black. What Mike Baker had given to Conner Braxton for eradicating the server that contained those incriminating documents, was now working its way through not just that one server, but through a large portion of servers on the eastern seaboard. Within the program there was code that enabled it to send itself to other networks via the address books in individual's E-mail accounts.

Mike Baker had designed it to do its work and then go to sleep, to go into a suspended animation. It was what some refereed to as an "*Easter Egg.*" It would hatch at a predetermined time or based on certain criteria that had to be met. Mike Baker not only wanted to destroy the information, he wanted to profit from the destruction process as well. The virus would do some initial damage, just enough to start a panic. This would allow Bytes Technologies to capitalize by marketing the cure.

He had established his fortune in much the same fashion. He treated business as though it was a war, a war that had no rules and had to be won at any cost. His reputation had evolved from a shy, unassuming nerd who dropped out of college to pursue his vision of the future, to that of a ruthless and cunning shark in the business community. He had stepped over his share of dead bodies to gain his position and stature. At first, he was able to charm those he hurt with his childlike mannerisms. Those charms no longer worked. They did not need to. Everyone knew who he was and what he was about. He closed the Web Page that brought him the news of the release of the worm.

He walked once again to his favorite place in front of the window in his office. Gazing out over the cityscape his smile broadened, and he reminded himself that the Dogwatch had earned a bonus. After all, he was about to rake in billions repairing what he had just destroyed.

They still had to find Lawrence, he remained a threat and his ultimate demise was the last piece of the puzzle. With Lawrence eliminated, the Group could move forward and begin its march into the new millennium. It was time to make the call.

Lawrence did not sleep at all that night. He spent his time watching television and moving from the sofa to the chair to his desk and back to the sofa. He carried the photograph with him, staring at it and looking for what he could have missed. He knew that he couldn't return to Rivermont. They would surely have increased security in light of his remodeling job. Those Country Club types would never stand for the desecration of their sanctuary. He went over every pixel on the photograph and replayed everything that he had seen in his mind, there was nothing. He couldn't believe that he couldn't find anything. He kept mumbling to himself over and over,

"What? What are you trying to tell me?" as he stared at the picture.

The sun broke through the blinds in the one room apartment, and he decided that he needed some fresh air and some coffee. He gathered his backpack, as well as the photo, and headed for the lobby. Still cautious, he waited and watched before exiting the building. He could hear the pitter patter of his landlady's feet as she scurried to the door to peer out her peephole and see who was leaving. He contemplated waving at her through her door, but reconsidered, opened the front door, and walked down the stairs.

He stood in front of his building and looked both ways before deciding to go the coffee shop directly across the street. It was familiar to him, and he had become a regular there. He checked his pocket for change and got a paper out of the machine before entering. Making his way to the booth at the rear of the little coffee shop, he placed his backpack on the seat opposite of him and removed his coat. As he sat down, he made eye contact with the waitress, and she walked towards him.

"You know, you've become one of my best customers and I don't even know your name. Normally I wouldn't care, but seein how you are so cute, and you tip so well…"

"Bob, just call me Bob. Sounds the same forwards and backwards," he said interrupting her.

"Well, just Bob, what can I get ya?" she said.

He paused for a moment to check her nametag and to decide if he felt like eating or not.

"Well Jennifer, I think I'll just have coffee this morning," he said.

"Just coffee? No bagel?" she replied.

"Yes, just coffee," he said.

"Well just Bob, I guess I will just pour the coffee."

She turned over the cup on the table and poured. She then winked at him and turned her attention to the other customers. He watched as she turned and left. She was young and attractive, and he thought she might have been flirting with him. This pleased him greatly. He felt normal for the first time in a long while. For just a brief moment, he was released from the nightmare that represented his current situation.

He opened the paper and began to read as he leisurely sipped on his coffee. He noted the paper was filled with the same old depressing news of crime, murder, and continued corruption. As he made his way through the paper, he found himself working on his third cup of coffee. He began reading an article on the life and times of a Presidential confidant.

What had caught his eye was not the article, but a picture that had accompanied the piece. It was a picture of Clay Danvers on the porch of his cabin. His dog was laying next to him while he sat in an old handcrafted rocking chair. Something bothered Lawrence about the image. His mind raced as he tried to focus in on exactly what that something was.

Frustration soon followed. It was like knowing the answer to something and having that answer right on the tip of your tongue. He continued to stare at the picture in the newspaper, and it finally hit him. He grabbed for his backpack and removed the photo that Danvers had sent to him just prior to his death. He set the photo next to the picture in the newspaper.

"That's it!" He exclaimed out loud.

Every head in the coffee shop turned in his direction, and just as quickly, they turned their attention back to their own little worlds. Lawrence remembered the small brass plaque on the side of the bathroom, which contained an etched picture of a log cabin and the name of the builder.

Clay was not trying to tell him to go to Rivermont. He was telling him that what he had left behind, what he had wanted Lawrence to find, had been at his cabin in the mountains. Lawrence even went so far as to speculate that the corner indicated on the photograph probably, corresponded with the location of whatever Clay had left behind.

Lawrence left $20 on the table, gathered his things, and bolted out of the coffee shop. He waved to Jennifer and told her to keep the change. He sprinted across the street and up the stairs to his apartment. As he entered the building, he almost ran over his landlady, apologizing as he spun her around and left her in his wake. Back inside the safety and confines of his apartment. He paced the floor talking, wildly to no one in particular trying to figure out his next move.


The working grunts of the Dogwatch were all gathered around a monitor in front of Jason Wheeler. Conner walked out of his office and towards the men.

"What do you have?" he asked.

"Well Sir, I think we have him. Here is a video stream taken off of an ATM camera located on the street just behind the building where the subject has an office. Watch very closely."

"Alright, I am watching. Can you please tell me what I am looking for?" Conner said.

"Ok, I'll run it again. Notice the guy passing the camera in the baseball cap. He seems to be somewhat nervous. He is stopping and starting and fidgeting with his hat and his jacket. He looks like he is uncomfortable in his own skin," Jason said.

"So, are you trying to tell me that is something out of the ordinary? Shit, I see that on a daily basis," Conner replied, knowing the answer, but wanting to hear it anyway.

"Ok, I'll give you that. Now look what happens as I freeze the frame."

Jason worked the mouse, connected to his computer like a master painter. He resized the frame. One hand was working the mouse and the other working the keyboard. The choppy, blurry video was transformed into a surprisingly clear close up of the man in question.

"Wheeler, you never cease to amaze even me. All right people, we are in business. Jason, make a print for everyone. I want you to hit the bricks, show this picture to every low life you can find, and see if we can get a match. Maybe we'll get lucky and get a fix on him."

The printer spit out copies of the pictures, and Jason handed a copy to each of his team members. He began to turn off his system and attempt to head out with the others, when Conner stopped him cold.

"Wheeler, you're with me."

Jason turned and tried to refrain from showing his emotion. He had hoped that the boss would keep him in house. After all, he did his best work in front of the computer.

"Have you had a chance to play with our new toy yet?" Conner asked.

"A little," he responded.

"But I hate to tell you, we aren't going to be able to use it," he continued.

"What do you mean?" asked Conner.

"It is in beta test right now, and they are basically using a mobile base for operations. We can't keep up with their location changes, and even if we could it is a proprietary system. There is no remote access to the system. Even if and when they launch the program and the base is at a fixed location, I doubt we will even be able to utilize it then," Jason said.

"And why not?"

"For the same reason. The system will still be a proprietary system, and access will, in all likelihood, be impossible from the outside. Think of it as a self-contained unit, no wires coming in and no wires going out. From the looks of it, the security counter measures are cutting edge, like nothing I have ever seen," Jason said.

"Just great," Conner responded in disgust.

"Do you have any other good news for me?" he said sarcastically.

"As a matter of fact I do. Remember the pain in the ass process we went through, going over his personal history and all? You know, phone records, grocery store purchases, and video rentals?" Jason said.

"Yes, so what?" Conner replied.

"One interesting thing popped up," Jason said.

"Ok, spill it," Conner replied.

"We ran all his purchases through a rather interesting filtering program I developed. What we were trying to find was any habit the subject expressed on a regular basis," Jason said.

"All right, all ready. Get to the punch line will you!" Conner said.

"Coffee." Jason replied.

"Coffee? What the hell are you saying?" Conner replied.

"You heard me, coffee," Jason said.

"I know you said coffee, but what the hell does that mean to me?" Conner said as his temper began to flare.

"Settle down Chief. Don't blow a gasket. He likes coffee. Check that, he loves coffee," Jason said.

"So, I love coffee too" Conner replied.

"I know, but you'll drink anything that resembles coffee. He likes a certain kind of coffee. A certain kind of coffee that is only sold in 4 stores in the metro DC area and served at only 2 coffee shops in the area," Jason said.

"And when were you going to tell me this?" Conner said.

"Well, I…" Jason began to say.

"Never mind. You mean we might find this guy based on the kind of coffee he drinks?" Conner said in shock.

"You got it Chief. It's some kind of special bean grown high on some Colombian mountain. I guess it's supposed to be bitter and pretty strong stuff," Jason said.

"Coffee, all this technology and we find our break in the kind of coffee this guy drinks. Man, that is just plain whacked.

Get the location of the stores and the coffee shops to the others. Tell them to show the picture around there, and see if we get a hit," Conner said.

"Yes Sir," Jason replied.

"And by the way," Conner said.

"Yes?" Jason relied.

"Good work young man," Conner said.

Jason didn't say another word, he simply turned towards his computer and smiled. Each of the team members had satellite phones with text messaging capabilities. Jason quickly typed in the new instructions on his keyboard and hit the send command.

Mike Baker had just finished reading the update Conner had sent via the encrypted Web Page. He was very pleased with the progress. Not only had the Dogwatch taken care of the documentation possessed by Lawrence, they now had a firm lead on his whereabouts. It was only a matter of time until the last remaining piece of this troublesome puzzle was found and the task at hand completed.

He sent instructions back to Conner telling him that once the subject had been located, to simply sit on him and not make a move. Mike was aware of the fact that there still existed the possibility that Lawrence had hard copies of his documentation. Despite his eagerness to terminate Lawrence, and end this, he wanted to make sure that all the bases were covered before disposing of him. He picked up his telephone and dialed.

"Hello?" a voice said on the other end.

"We need to meet. Be at my office 7:00 tonight, and don't be late," Mike said.

"All right," responded the voice on the other end.

And the line went dead.

Mike Baker was about to use the ace he had hidden up his sleeve. A card he knew he would eventually have to expose and use. He never made apologies for using whatever means necessary to guarantee the results he desired. He was a true believer in doing whatever it took, and this was no exception. He looked at this option as preventative medicine or an insurance policy. He never knew if he was going to need it, but it was better to be prepared, than to be without options.


The excitement of the day's events was long gone. Lawrence was deep in thought as to how to proceed. He had to leave town, which didn't bother him in the slightest. The trip to Clay's mountain retreat was relatively long, and he knew that he would have to drive. He figured that he would have to visit his newfound friend and entrepreneur, Lucky. He needed to return the car he had used and trade it in for something that fit in better in that type of terrain. He also needed to obtain certain items that would make his treasure hunting a bit easier.

As he began to jot down the items he needed, his thoughts drifted towards Kelly. He wondered if she was safe and whether she had made it out of town. He wondered if she missed him as much as he missed her? He decided to call her mother's to see if she had made it. He wanted to assure her that he was all right and that he missed her. He wanted to tell her that everything was going to be all right, and that this would all be over very soon. He picked up the phone and dialed.

"Hello?" Kelly's mother answered.

"Mrs. Ford, this is Lawrence, is Kelly there?" he asked.

"Why no dear. Is she supposed to be?" she replied.

"No, I just thought she might be," he said as the concern showed in his voice.

"Is everything all right? You sound upset, Dear Boy."

"Yes, everything is fine."

"As a matter of fact, I will just try her at home," he continued.

"Now listen here young man, we haven't seen you in some time. When are you going to honor us with a visit?"

"Soon Mrs. Ford, real soon. Work has kept me so busy and confused that I need a break, if you couldn't tell. I promise that I will get up there as soon as possible"

"I am going to hold you to that. I expect to see you soon."

"Ok Mrs. Ford, just as soon as I clear my desk of the project I am working on."

Lawrence had to laugh at that statement. His current project was staying alive, while toppling the Government. Just another typical day in his life, he thought.

"Wonderful, and please stop with the Mrs. Ford. You are practically family my Dear Boy. Just call me Mum, will you?"

"Yes Mrs. Ford, and we will see you soon."

"All right, bye dear. Give Kelly my love, and tell her she needs to call her poor mother more often."

Lawrence hung the phone up and immediately began to pace. He realized that maybe they had tapped her parents phone. He was also worried because he had told Kelly to leave town, to go and visit her mother. He thought that maybe she had possibly gone somewhere else, but where? Rather that torture himself with the where and why, he decided the best thing to do would be to page her. He did miss her, and talking to her might calm his already fragile nerves. Not wanting to page her from his apartment, he decided to use the payphone on the corner, he was not going to risk it again.

His anxiety had not given way to his paranoia. He made his way to the lobby and then down the stairs, following the same routine. After a brief moment, he was out the door and walking to the corner.

He dialed the number and entered the payphones number after the obligatory tone. Standing at the payphone, leaning against it he had visions of torturous and evil men doing unthinkable things to Kelly. He tried to forgive himself for putting her in the middle of all of this. Then the phone rang.

"Kelly?" he said.

"Peanut?" she responded.

"Where are you now?" he asked.

"At home," she replied sheepishly.

"What the hell are you doing? I thought I told you to go to your mother's and wait," he shouted into the phone.

"I am so sorry. I was scared. You left in such a hurry, I didn't know what to think, let alone what to do," she said.

"I know, and I am sorry I had to leave in such a hurry. It's just…" he was interrupted.

"I have to see you Lawrence," she blurted out.

149

Lawrence, he thought, she called me Lawrence. He couldn't remember the last time she called him Lawrence. He knew she was upset, and he contemplated taking her with him to the mountains. She might be safer with him, especially since they would be leaving town.

"Kelly, I want you to listen to me, I am leaving town tomorrow, and I want you to come with me. I want you to be ready to go in the morning. I will page you and let you know where and when to meet me," he said.

"But Peanut, I need to talk to you…" she was interrupted.

"We will have plenty of time to talk. I have to go. Wait for my page, and I'll see you soon. I promise everything will be clearer in the morning," he said.

"But…"

"No buts. Wait for my call. I love you Kelly," he said as he hung the phone up.

Lawrence leaned on the phone booth as he placed the receiver back in its cradle. He was relieved that she was safe and that she would soon be reunited with him. He hoped he was making the right decision. He hoped he wasn't being selfish and thinking only of his needs. He knew he had time to rethink his decision, to clear his head, and let logic enter into the equation.

He turned and slowly walked back to his apartment. As he walked, he realized that he had uttered those three words. He felt better knowing that he had said it. He hoped that it wasn't lost in the confusion of the moment.

Kelly sat at the foot of her bed, the phone still at her ear. She gently set the receiver down while saying,

"I need to tell you something…"

The tears came slowly at first, followed by an uncontrollable sob. She realized that she missed him, and that she needed him. It was not long after, that she began to realize that she truly loved him as well.

She walked towards the bathroom and stood in front of the mirror. Cocking her head from side to side, she looked at her reflection, focusing in on her eyes. Her stare seemed to increase in its intensity as she tried to look deep inside herself through those eyes. But she had no time for this now. She had a meeting to get to. She broke off the soul searching for the moment and proceeded to get dressed.

Nathan drew the side of town that had one grocery store and one of the coffee shops that served the brand of coffee Lawrence happened to fancy. He struck out at the grocery store. None of the employees recognized the man in the photograph. He then made his way to the coffee shop.

It was a quaint little establishment, very trendy. The motif seemed to be reminiscent of the brand of coffee shops popular on the West Coast. The type of place where you might imagine poets come to recite their work after-hours or where a musician might break out his or her guitar and play a little something they just wrote. The first person he bumped into was a cute little number named Jennifer.

"Have you ever seen this guy?" He said as he stuck the picture in her face.

"Easy Rambo, who wants to know?"

"Listen lady, I don't want any trouble. Just answer the question," he said as he produced his fake credentials.

"My brother got one of those at a gag shop down the street," she said as she examined the badge.

His stare became increasingly intense and she seemed to lose the sarcastic look on her face. He placed the badge back in his jacket, she caught a glimpse of the gun that was holstered underneath his jacket.

"Listen, I don't want any trouble. Sure, I've seen the guy. He comes in every morning for coffee and a bagel. Sometimes, he comes in twice a day," she said.

"Has he been in today?" he asked.

"Sure, like clockwork, practically every morning. He sat back there, in the same place he sits every time," she replied.

"Now that wasn't too difficult, was it?" he replied as he turned to leave.

"He isn't in any kind of trouble, is he? I mean he seems like such a nice guy," she said

"No, he isn't in any kind of trouble. However, I would appreciate it if you wouldn't mention my visit if he happens to return again. I mean, you wouldn't want any trouble would you?"

"If he comes back, I would appreciate it if you would call me," he said as he reached into his jacket to retrieve a card and expose his holstered weapon once again.

She didn't speak. She just shook her head and indicated that she understood. Nathan turned to leave retrieving his phone from his jacket pocket as he walked. Once safely outside, he dialed the command center.

"Conner, it's Nathan."

# Chapter - - 18

Mike Baker picked up the phone and was informed that he had a guest at the garage entrance.

"Its okay Sam, they're expected. I am sorry I didn't phone you to inform you of the anticipated arrival," he said.

He hung the phone up and arose from his chair to turn and face the window once again. He loved that window and the view. He loved to give his guests the perception that he was surveying all that was his. He heard the elevator as it chimed, and then he heard the doors slide open and the gentle sound of footsteps as they made their way towards his office. The door opened and he spoke. There was no need to turn around.

"Glad to see you could join me this evening, Kelly. It has been a long time, and I have missed you so. Can I offer you something to drink?"

Lawrence needed a break. His emotions were working over time, and his judgement was impaired. He needed to escape, if only for a moment. He turned on his computer. As it was going through its booting process, he turned on the television. Surfing through the channels, he ended up on GNN.

He didn't much care for television. He mainly stayed with educational programs and the occasional news programs. His attention was immediately drawn towards the television, and he hit the volume button. He watched and listened as the lead story was about a new virus that had infected several network systems.

The source and strength of the virus was yet to be determined, but the effect was devastating. Apparently, it was only affecting a small number of systems that seemed to be tied to the same network. The effect was total failure to any system that was infected. The problem was confirmed on the East Coast and was feared to be spreading worldwide.

Lawrence was somewhat concerned and turned his attention to his computer. The boot process had finished, and he moved his mouse over the Internet icon on his desktop. He held his finger over the button. He waited and contemplated the possibility that the bug might infect his system. Curiosity got the best of him, and with a single click, he accessed the Internet.

He waited as the dial tone finished, and the series of tones began the back and forth communication. The screen flickered, and then a page appeared that informed him that the page he had requested was not available. He hit the icon for his mailbox and waited. His mail program finished downloading, and he hit the outgoing mail button. He had to do this to access the documentation he had set in the send function.

When the dialogue box appeared asking him for a password and then asking if he wanted to send it now or at a later time and date, he simply set the send function for 24 hours later. If he didn't access it within 24 hours, it would automatically send. That was his safeguard. What he didn't realize was that the information was gone and that the files had already been compromised. His insurance policy was gone.

That dialogue box he was accustomed to seeing never appeared. Instead, the laptop seemed to slow down. Then the screen began to display rows and rows of meaningless jargon. He quickly yanked the phone connection from his computer, but it was too late. His computer now had a worm virus that was making its way through his hard drive turning all his files into a series of meaningless numbers and letters.

He leaned back in his chair and looked at the ceiling. His mouth was wide open. He feared the worse. He had lost his insurance policy. He found himself in the position of having no protection from his enemies. He had failed to keep hard copies of his documentation. He had feared that keeping such things could only lead to trouble. He had banked on technology, and it had failed him.

Steadily the paranoia that seemed to occupy his life began to creep back in. Did they know about his so-called insurance policy? Had they been responsible for this? Did this mean they were close? He was in full panic mode now. All he had was a picture sent to him by Clay Danvers, and its significance had yet to be determined. Wait a minute, he thought. He had copied his information to a floppy. At the time, he was just being weird, paranoid, but now… Where had he put it? He tore the small apartment apart in a mad effort to locate the disk.

"Got it!" He said as he pulled the disk from a zippered pocket in his backpack.

He kissed the disk and for a brief moment felt relief. All hope was not yet lost. Even if he didn't find anything at Clay's mountain retreat, he still had his original information. He had no computer, but he had the information. A computer would just go on the list of items he would ask Lucky to obtain. Realizing that the hour was late, he grabbed his backpack and headed for the door. His next stop was Lucky's Rentown.

Kelly was sitting in a chair opposite Mike Baker, who was now seated and facing her. She was staring at him with great contempt, wondering how it was she had gotten here. She had a promising career with the FBI at one point in time. She had been assigned to the Justice Department as part of an ongoing investigation into the business practices of Bytes Technologies and specifically, Mike Baker. That was when her career suffered a tremendous setback.

Through a series of bad decisions and the lure of a rich and successful man, she found herself the scapegoat of an investigation gone bad. The Justice Department had blown its investigation apart. They had failed in their attempt to break up Bytes monopoly on the software market.

What she didn't know, what she may never know, is that the investigation was doomed from the beginning. She was just a pawn in a vicious game that had to have a winner and a loser. The outcome of the investigation was a lock for Mike Baker. The administration just needed someone to take the fall. That someone was Kelly. The incident was kept out of the press, and she was quietly dismissed. Bytes suffered through some fines and court time, but the outcome was that they remained on top and in charge.

Out of work and finished within the intelligence community, she ended up in the bed and in the employ of Mike Baker. She had served him well over the years, and her introduction to Lawrence Brazelton was no coincidence. The Group had wanted to simply eliminate him, but had succumbed to the wishes of the President and spared his life. So Kelly was brought in to keep him in the family, to make sure of his every move.

Kelly knew that from the moment she had seen Clay Danvers at Lawrence's home right before his death that the piper was coming to collect. And so she sat and stared, waiting for Mike to speak. He finally broke the silence.

"Why so quiet my dear? And that look."

"Why am I here?" she asked.

"Simple, you work for me, or have you forgotten? I want you to remember that all you have, your home, clothes, car, are all paid for by me," he said.

"And all that I don't have, I owe to you as well," she replied.

"Touché my dear, touché. However, let us get to the reason you are here. We seem to have lost our Mr. Brazelton, or shall I call him Peanut?" he said.

"You Bastard!" she replied.

"Now, now, such harsh words coming from such a lovely mouth. Here is what I want. When your Peanut calls you in the morning…"

"How did you know?"

"You have my house wired you Son of a Bitch!" she said as she cut him off mid sentence.

The stare intensified and the tremendous hatred she had fostered for so long continued to rage within her. Kelly had concluded some time ago that in all probability her home was bugged, but the reality of it incensed her. She managed to maintain her composure and continued listening to the egotistical diatribe Mike was engaged in.

"As I was saying, when he calls you, will meet him. What I am interested in is certain information that may be in his possession, information that he might wish to share with a certain rather nosey Special Prosecutor. I would like to know if he still has this information, and I would also like to know what he intends to do with it," he said.

"I have been with this man for over a year, and I have never heard him mention anything that resembles what you are referring to. What makes you think he is going to say anything now?" she said.

"Let's call it a gut instinct, as well as timing. Now I don't want you to get any ideas, you will have company on this little venture. They will have instructions to terminate both of you, with, how do you say, oh yes, extreme prejudice, if they feel the situation is not moving in the proper direction," he said.

"What makes you feel like I will even go along with this? You're going to kill him anyway, and more than likely your going to kill me as well," she said.

Mike let the question hang in the air for a moment. It was all part of his controlling personality. He did it often, and it seemed to have the right effect. Kelly began to squirm slightly in her seat, at which point Mike answered her.

"Incentive my dear, and the proper motivation to help you see things more clearly. By the way, how are your parents these days? Is Dad enjoying retirement? I bet Mum has a lovely garden. Pity if anything were to happen to them before they could enjoy the benefits of those glorious golden years," he said.

"You Son of a Bitch!" she barked.

"Perhaps, but I think you understand how serious I am about this," he said as he reached into his desk and handed a small box to Kelly.

"What the hell is this?" she asked.

"Inside you will find a rather stylish broach. It is equipped with a small camera and microphone. You will wear it for your little rendezvous tomorrow. You didn't think I would let you just waltz in and warn our friend of your intentions now did you?" he said.

"I guess not. Playing fair is beyond you." she replied.

"Now if you take care of this little problem for me and I get what I want, you can have what you want, your freedom and enough money to keep you happy for three lifetimes. Mum and Dad can live out their lives, and everyone will be happy," he said.

Kelly sat in silence and gazed at the box. Emotions were coursing through her body. She loved Lawrence. It wasn't supposed to have happened, but it had. She feared for the life of her parents. She knew that Mike Baker was capable of doing horrible things, but this? She looked up into the cold eyes of her employer.

"Deal," she said.

Without another word, she got up and walked out of the office. She had just made a deal with the Devil, and her heart ached with the pain of a thousand tortured souls. Mike watched as Kelly walked towards the door. The short skirt and high heels had his imagination churning. The way she carried herself drove him nuts. He thought to himself that he never should have put her in the field. He should have kept her for himself.

He turned his attention towards his computer. After he had completed the update of the Web Page, which contained the instructions for the morning's events, he sat back and lit one his favorite Cuban Cigars. With his feet on the desk, he cocked his head back and began to blow smoke rings towards the ceiling. Nothing beat the flavor of an exceptional cigar and the feeling of an impending victory. Everything seemed to be falling into place. Mike Baker was indeed the king of all he surveyed.

Conner had just finished talking with Nathan in the field. He had instructed him to stay put and monitor the area. He had given Jason instructions to have the others converge on Nathan's position and wait. He headed to his office to contact their employer.

As he brought the Web Page up, he noticed that it had changed, so he ran it through the encryption process and began to read. That tricky bastard, he thought to himself. Things began to be much clearer now. His employer's confidence was rooted in the knowledge that he had an asset on the inside, a sleeper.

His instructions were simple, pick up surveillance of the girl at her home and tail her in the morning. Let her know that you are there, and follow her to her meeting with Brazelton. He provided Conner with the frequency for the mini-cam she would be wearing. Both Mike Baker and Conner could watch the meeting in the safety of their respective offices. They were to await instructions once in place. Conner decided that the team deserved a break, so he instructed them all to return to the warehouse. He would sit on the woman until morning and give the men a much-deserved night off.

Lawrence made his way to the Mercedes sedan he had parked in a garage several blocks from his apartment. His paranoia seemed to intensify with each passing moment. His thoughts drifted to his anticipated reunion with Kelly. He reminded himself that the reason this whole thing started was due to his relationship with her. As he drove through the streets of the city, his mind was actively engaged with everything that had transpired over the last few days. His thoughts almost distracted him from making the turn into the Lucky's Rentown. He hit the brakes hard and made a sharp turn into the lot.

Once inside the back gate, he sat in the vehicle and waited for Lucky to make his appearance. It didn't take long. Lucky appeared moments after Lawrence's arrival. He walked towards the Mercedes with his arms extended and a rather cheesy smile plastered on his face.

"My friend, so good to see you. Although I didn't expect to see you so soon," Lucky said.

"Yeah, good to see you as well. Listen I need another favor," Lawrence said as he handed a piece of paper to Lucky.

"Rather interesting shopping list my friend. Are you going hunting?" Lucky said.

"Yeah, hunting. Can you fill it?" Lawrence asked.

"For you, my best customer and new friend, no problem. When?"

"Tomorrow, early AM. Is that a problem?" Lawrence said.

"Could be, but I think I can handle it. You understand that even though I consider you a close friend and all, the arrangement is still C.O.D. I think I can have you packed and ready to go by 9:00am," Lucky said.

"Yeah, I understand. Just make it happen, and I will make it worth your while. And 9:00 will be just fine." Lawrence said.

"Ah, the language I love so dearly. I will see you in the morning," Lucky said.

Lawrence turned and walked through the gate and past the old rusted out cars on the front lot. He made his way down the street, sat on a bench, and waited for the next bus. After a series of transfers and cab rides, he arrived at his apartment. Standing on the corner, observed the comings and goings on the street. Nothing seemed out of the ordinary, except for one man.

Lawrence waited and watched the man as he moved from side to side, all the while looking and watching, much the same as Lawrence did. Fearing the worst, Lawrence made his way to the little coffee shop across the street from his apartment. He quickly and quietly ducked inside, but rather than take the booth in the rear, he took a seat in the front. He watched the man as he paced back and forth.

"Can I get you some coffee?"

Somewhat startled Lawrence turned to see Jennifer standing beside him with a coffeepot and a smile. His heart rate returned to a more normal rhythm.

"Sure," he responded.

He turned again to face the window and continued to observe the man. As he watched, the man reached into his pocket and produced a rather interesting phone. He talked only for a moment and then turned and left. Lawrence seemed to relax a bit, as he figured his paranoia was making him draw some pretty unrealistic conclusions.

What Lawrence didn't see was that three other men had received calls on similar phones and were now departing from their locations nearby. Feeling a little better, he turned his attention back to Jennifer.

"I think I'll have a bagel as well," he said.

Jennifer didn't acknowledge him. She simply looked at him. He could tell that something was wrong, but he wasn't sure exactly what it could be. She had a look of confusion on her face. Finally, she broke her silence.

"Some guy was in here asking about you today," she said.

Lawrence's face froze, and he found himself temporarily paralyzed. Seconds seemed to become hours. He tried to speak, but found that his words were stuck somewhere between his larynx and mouth. He fought through the fear and the paralysis and was able to get out only a single word.

"What?"

"Yeah, a guy came in today with a picture. He was asking around to see if anyone had seen the guy in the picture. He had a badge and everything. He was pretty intense, if you know what I mean. When he got around to me, I told him that I had seen you before. You're not in any kind of trouble are you?" she said.

Lawrence had half listened to what was coming out of her mouth, using the time to gather his composure. He forced a smile over his lips and attempted a look of carelessness.

"Me, in trouble? No," he said.

"The man said if I see you, I should give him a call. He said it would be in my best interest and all. He gave me this card," she said.

"Are you going to call him?" Lawrence asked.

She paused and looked at Lawrence before answering him.

"Nah, you look like an honest man and I hate those government pricks. You are one of my best customers. Why would I want to screw that up? I'll go and get your bagel," she said.

Lawrence turned first to the window, then back to Jennifer. His stomach was in knots. Someone had found him, but whom? The card Jennifer showed him had only a name and a phone number on it. How had they found him? Did they trace Kelly's call to the payphone? Did they have a tap on her mother's phone? He figured that if they had come this far, they surely had to know where his apartment was. He began to go over what he had left in the apartment. Had he left anything behind that could be damaging, that could lead them anywhere? He checked his backpack, and everything important to him was there. The only thing he had left behind was his laptop and it had been infected with some sort of virus.

The virus. He had thought the virus to be some sort of quirk. They had planted it, and that meant that they were closing in on not only him, but they had also found out what he had, and they had destroyed it. His mind was awash in chaos. If they felt like

161

they had accomplished their goal of destroying his information, they would be comfortable with terminating him.

Kelly's face crept into his thoughts. She was in danger now. Obviously they knew of his involvement with her, and that is how they had found him. The ironic twist that fate brings began to haunt him. He had begun this whole thing in an effort to protect her and to have a future with her. Now, he realized that rather than protect her he had signed her death warrant.

He didn't wait for his bagel. He left a $50 dollar bill on the table and made his way to the back of the coffee shop and out the rear entrance into the alley. He couldn't wait until morning. He had to get to Kelly now.


Conner watched as the last of the team arrived back at the warehouse. He broke out a case of beer and began to toss one to each of the men. As they began to sit around the conference table, you could hear the wisp of the aluminum cans as they were being opened.

"Gentlemen, first I want to thank you for a job well done," Conner said as he raised a can above his head in a toast.

"I realize that I can be an asshole at times, but I do appreciate your efforts."

"Tomorrow is going to be a busy day, so tonight I want you guys to rest, get drunk, or get laid. I don't give a shit," he said with a smile.

"We have an asset that will be meeting with the target tomorrow. This asset is one that I personally was unaware of. It seems as though our employer had the foresight to plant a sleeper. The sleeper just happens to be his girlfriend."

"That hotty works for us? Ouch! That hurts, don't it," remarked Victor.

"Our assignment is almost finished. We will provide surveillance for tomorrow's meet, and we will eliminate the subject once we get the green light. I want you all back here at 0600 hours tomorrow. Until then, your time is yours to do with as you please," Conner said.

"What are you going to do Chief?" asked Nathan.

"Baby-sit the sleeper. Now get outta here will ya, before I change my mind."

Conner watched as the men grabbed the remaining beer in the case and walked towards the door. He was pleased to see Jason accompanying them. He had worried that the others would not accept Jason. That fear was being relieved at the sight of the men as they left as a team. He knew that they had to have some fun before tomorrow's events. Even the most hardened killer needed to relax. He had decided to remain behind and be the one to watch over Kelly.

Their employer was not fully convinced of her loyalties and wanted to make sure that she was kept honest. After gathering a few things from his office and filling a thermos with coffee, he made his way to the large sliding door of the warehouse. This assignment was reaching its climax, and for that he was grateful. He needed a vacation, and after this was done, he would take one, possibly a permanent one.

# Chapter - - 19

Lawrence could not wait to see Kelly. As he made his way towards her house, he wondered if he was making a mistake in trying to see her. He had to remind himself that the only reason he had even traveled down this road was to have a future and more specifically to have a future with her. He found himself standing on the corner adjacent to her house.

To make sure the area was free of surveillance, he began a methodical visual sweep of the area. After he had checked all the cars, as well as all the pedestrians, he simply watched. People came and went. They waited for the coveted parking spots, carrying groceries and having conversations.

After about 20 minutes, he had noted that none of the people who were there when he arrived were there any longer. He made his way across the street and towards the rear of Kelly's brownstone, careful to note any new arrivals. He made his way up the back stairs and knocked on the screen door. He waited for what seemed to be forever, and just as his anxiety level began to rise, the door opened.

"You're more beautiful than I remembered," he said.

"Lawrence?" she replied as she looked passed him, as well as around him.

"What are you doing here?" she said as he entered. She closed the door behind him.

"I want to say it's because I missed you so badly, but that would only cover about half of it. I was worried about you, but I think they found me and…." he was interrupted.

"Worried about what, and who found you?" she said.

"Which phone did you call me from?" he asked.

"The one in the living room," she replied.

Lawrence walked through the kitchen and directly to the phone on the sofa table. He removed the receiver and unscrewed the mouth and earpiece, there was nothing. He grabbed the cord and followed it to the wall. Looking at the jack on the base of the wall, he removed a Swiss army knife from his pocket and quickly removed the two screws that held it to the wall. He gently pulled the jack from the wall and revealed a small bugging device attached to the jack.

Looking up at Kelly, he put his fingers to his lips and motioned for her to follow him. He rose and walked towards the back door. They found themselves right back where they had started.

"I think that is how they found me. You are not safe here. We have to go, and we have to leave now!" he said.

"But…" she was interrupted.

"We have no time for small talk. They have probably wired your entire house, and they probably know I am here now. We have to go!" he said.

Without another word, Kelly turned and walked back into the house. She put on some tennis shoes and grabbed a small bag she kept packed for overnights when she stayed at his house. When she returned to the back porch, she saw Lawrence carefully checking the surrounding area. She had left her lights on, as well as the television, to give the appearance that the house was occupied.

Quickly they made their way to the alley and towards the street. Once on the street, they turned and walked in the opposite direction of her brownstone.

Conner arrived just moments after their departure. He parked on the opposite side of the street from her brownstone. From his position, he could see that the lights were on, and he figured that he might as well settle in for the long haul.

He poured himself a cup of coffee from the thermos and relaxed. He figured that he didn't have much to worry about. She was on their team, and the target had no knowledge of that fact, or the fact that this was all going to be over tomorrow. And so, the wait began.

Lawrence had scouted out a seedy little motel on the poor side of town. The kind of place where nobody asked questions and rooms were rented by the hour rather than by the night. He paid the attendant in cash, never making eye contact with him. The attendant threw a key towards him and informed him that if he wanted clean sheets that it would be an extra $10 dollars. Lawrence declined the added perk.

Once inside the room, Kelly sat on the foot of the disgusting and oft used bed. Lawrence drew the shades, and for a brief moment, the room went dark. Lawrence turned on the lamp next to the bed and looked over at Kelly. In the dim light he could see that she was crying. He walked over to her and sat down. He reached around her and drew her head towards his shoulder.

"I will explain all of this I promise," he said.

"You don't understand, I…"

Lawrence cut her off before she could finish.

"Listen to me. This will all be over soon. I had hoped that you wouldn't be involved, but I guess my hope fell short."

"But I need to tell you something," she said.

"All I want you to do right now is listen," he said.

"But…" she began to say as Lawrence placed his finger gently over her lips.

"Listen," he said.

She looked up at him, and for some reason she didn't try to speak. She felt the sincerity in his voice and in the soft touch of his finger to her mouth. After a brief moment, he removed his finger from her soft lips and gently kissed her swollen lips. It was not a kiss in the heat of passion. It was a kiss filled with love and comfort. Slowly he rose and began to speak. She sat and listened.

"When I first graduated from Law School, I was hired by a rather small but prestigious firm. I was young, cocky, and full of life. I had a beautiful wife and a new baby. I worked my ass off, passed the bar on my first try, and scored the highest in my group. My life was going just as I had planned, and it wasn't long before I made partner. I had brought in a lot of clients, and coupled with my billable hours, I was making the firm a truckload of cash. My attitude grew along with my bank account, and I felt like I could do whatever pleased me. I got caught up in the excesses of the 70's. Experimented with drugs and my sexuality. I didn't think it would matter all that much, after all, I was the golden child. Little did I know that the sins of the past would and could be used against me."

167

"Not long after my arrival into the firm, a brash, charismatic young attorney joined the firm. I knew him indirectly from my college days, and set up the interview at the firm. It was more or less a favor for another college friend. The new recruit had a bright and promising future. His was not the greatest legal mind, but he had a charm, a way with people. His legal decisions and choice of clients eventually caused the firm to come under some pressure. His life was destined for something greater than the legal profession, and important clients of the firm had pegged him for public service."

"Preston Wesley?" she interjected.

"Yep, the President of the United States. He was in the exploratory stages of a political run. The firm needed this run to be successful. Not just for its own selfish motives, but also for the motives of the real power in politics, the money and the people with the money. Most of which happened to be clients of the firm. To make a long story short, I was offered as the sacrificial lamb. Wesley had taken on a new client, and this client had serious mob ties. How would it look for a blooming political candidate to have had dealings with the Mafia?" he said.

"But how did you get so tied up in all of this?" she asked.

"My past. I had been doing a mixture of drugs one night at a party and got into a situation that involved a young man and his wife. I don't think I need to draw you a picture of what transpired."

There was an awkward silence as both Kelly and Lawrence tried not to paint individual mental pictures. Kelly closed her eyes and continued to listen patiently as Lawrence continued.

"It happened once, and since that time, I have worked on cleaning up my act, as well as my marriage at the time. Hell, every partner was crazy back then. At any rate, that singular event turned my world into the shit storm of today. Rather than suffer the embarrassment I was facing, I agreed to be the fall guy. I had the guarantees of a good future, plenty of money, and hell, it's not like I was going to prison. I was just facing a life without the one thing I enjoyed, being an attorney. We altered all the documentation pertaining to Wesley's involvement with

168

the Cordona family to reflect the decisions and actions as my sole responsibility."

Kelly could tell by his expressions that Lawrence was conflicted about how he should feel. She could see the sorrow for wasting his talent. She could also see the anger he harbored for his enemies.

"For Wesley the problem was gone, for me the nightmare had begun. All the original documentation was destroyed, or so he thought. I had made copies and had kept them as a sort of insurance policy. Both my wife and son are dead, and while I can't prove that it was the work of Wesley and the men that pull his strings, it doesn't mean I don't know it was them," he said.

"But why?" she asked.

"I have no idea. It makes absolutely no sense to me. My best guess is to keep me quiet. They didn't know I still had the original documentation. I suppose they figured if I had something, they couldn't risk killing me. Instead, they stripped me of everything I had, and like an idiot, I kept taking my licks. But that's the past. I am not risking another life due to the weakness of my character, not again," he said.

"What life? What are you talking about?" she asked.

"Yours," he replied.

"I am finally happy. I never thought I would be happy again. I never thought I would love someone again. With you, I have found someone I want to share the rest of my life with, grow old with. Hell, I am old, but you know what I mean. Until this is over, we can't have peace. I will always be looking over my shoulder waiting for the worst to happen. I love you Kelly, and I want to be with you, but until this is over, and I mean finally over, that's not possible."

Lawrence paused and walked to the window. He drew the curtain back slightly and looked out, continuing to relate his story to Kelly.

"That is why we are here. I contacted the office of the Independent Counsel. We met and discussed the terms for the release of the information I might be in possession of. Somehow they found out, Clay warned me right before he died. My plan has taken a lot of side streets to this point, but I know that given

169

a couple of days, we can have this all behind us.  The reason I came for you is that they have found out what I have, and they think that they have destroyed it.  But I have a copy, and until this is over, I am afraid that they may use you to get to me.  They need to be certain that their mess is all cleaned up before they take me out.  And believe me, I am not ready to go, not yet, and not without a fight," he said.

Kelly looked deep into his eyes, directly into his soul.  She could see that he was filled with passion, as well as commitment.  She had hit a crossroads in her life.  She had taken the assignment in the beginning as just that, an assignment.  Time had corrupted her judgment and clouded it.  She began to fall for the man that she had been assigned to observe.  Fallen so far that she found herself in love with him.

She felt sorrow and compassion for him and the life that had been forced on him.  It was not fair that one man should suffer so much at the hands of men who care so little for others.  Kelly found her love and respect for Lawrence grew as she realized the extent of his suffering and his commitment to her.  He was willing to sacrifice his own life and the comforts of what little existence he had for her.

The choice she was about to make would be a defining moment in her life.  Lives hung in the balance. The lives of Lawrence, her parents, as well as herself, sat silently in the background, unaware that her decision would be of any consequence.

She reached into her purse and removed the small box that contained the mini- cam she was to wear for tomorrow's meeting.

"Lawrence, I want you to know that I love you.  Nothing would please me more than to grow old with you.  I support any decision you make.  I have something to tell you as well, but I wanted to say that first.  I wanted you to hear those words before I say what I have to say," she said.

She paused and gathered her thoughts.  It was now her turn to stand, her turn to speak the words that would either unite them or divide them.  She hoped that he would understand.

"I work for them," she said.

"What!" he said.

The word shot out of his mouth as more of a reflex than a complete understanding of what was taking place. It took a moment for him to truly grasp what he had just heard.

"What are you saying?" he said.

She opened the small box and handed it to him. Lawrence took the box and removed the broach. Underneath it was a small power source, transmitte,r and the wires for connecting it to the mini cam. Lawrence held the broach in front of him.

"What is this?" he asked.

"A camera and microphone I was supposed to wear for our meeting tomorrow. It was given to me by the men that are looking for you," she said.

Lawrence felt all of the strength leave his body. His legs buckled, and he collapsed onto the bed, still clutching the small box and broach.

"Not you, why?" he asked.

"It's not that simple. They threatened my parents, they threatened my damn parents!" she said.

Lawrence gathered enough energy to stand as he made his way to the small table in the corner of the room.

"They threatened your parents?" he said.

"It's more complicated than that," she replied.

"I'm listening," he said.

"I am no different than you. I had a life before you, a promising life. I made some bad choices and wound up in bed with the wrong man, the same man who is directing this witch-hunt for you. In the beginning, I was brought in to keep tabs on you, to feed them any information that seemed relevant. After a while, it was apparent you were happy with your life and that you were not a threat. You have to understand that I could have left a long time ago. I chose to stay with you because I was falling in love with you. You have to believe that!"

"Believe? You expect me to believe you?"

"Yes, I thought things were over. I hadn't heard from them in some time. I knew something was wrong when Clay showed up that day," she said.

"Why didn't you tell me then?" he asked.

"I don't know. Everything happened so fast. Clay died, you were acting weird, and then you just left. I was confused, and I didn't know what to do," she said.

"And what am I supposed to think now?" he asked.

"Know this, I love you, and I want to help you. I know you are pissed as hell, and I don't blame you, but I need you to trust me. I didn't have to tell you about the plans for tomorrow's meeting. I didn't have to show you the camera. Look at me, can't you see that I love you?" she said.

Lawrence was still looking at the small broach. He slowly raised his head and looked at Kelly. She was crying. Her face expressed the pain and anguish she was going through. He looked deep into her eyes, to the point where the soul is perched waiting to be seen. He saw the light in her eyes. Through all the tears and through all the pain, he saw the honesty in her. Without another moment's hesitation, he rose to his feet and walked towards her with his arms extended. He took her in his arms and drew her close to his chest.

"I trust you," he whispered into her ear.

"I trust you."

With those words, the floodgates opened, and she began to sob uncontrollably. He held her tightly and gently stroked her hair as he kissed her on the side of the head. He spent the next several minutes letting her deal with her confession, as well as her emotions.

While she cleansed her soul with a good cry in the arms of a man who had exhibited the ultimate trust, he was busy contemplating his next move in this game of chess. That evening's revelations had put him in full control of his own destiny, providing he made the proper choices. To them he was the hunted, but in reality, he was now the hunter.

Lawrence sat in the corner of the room holding the small broach, twirling it in his fingers. He stopped for a moment and glanced towards the bed. Kelly was curled up in a ball, fully clothed, and she appeared to be sleeping. He wouldn't press her for any of the gritty details that had brought her to this point in her life. That discussion was for a different time and place. All he cared about now was that she had come clean and that she was here with him.

He returned his attention to the small technological marvel in his hand. It was at that moment, he realized he could protect Kelly, give them what they wanted, and buy enough time to find out the mystery of the photograph Clay had sent him. He carefully returned the items to the small box and walked over towards Kelly.

"Honey, time to go," he said as he gently shook her.

"What? Go? Go where?" she said in a raspy voice looking at him through bloodshot eyes.

"I have a plan. I need you to trust me. If you do, everything will be fine. You will be safe, your parents will be safe, and they will get what is coming to them. Come on," he said as he walked towards the door.

Without hesitation, she got up and followed him through the door. Lawrence walked into the lobby and tossed the key to the attendant. They walked towards the street and hailed a cab.

"We have one stop to make before you go back home," he said.

"Home?" she said.

"Remember, I said you have to trust me," he replied.

For the next 30 minutes, they drove in complete silence, each one looking out their window, all the while holding hands tightly. The driver pulled up to the curb, and Lawrence paid him.

"What are we doing at your office?" Kelly asked.

"All part of the plan. You have to trust me," he said.

He walked into the building full of confidence. He had no fear of the men he was trying so hard to evade. He was reasonably confident that they wouldn't be anywhere near his office. They were more than likely outside of his apartment.

As they exited the elevator, Lawrence began to unfold his plan. Kelly seemed hesitant and expressed fear that he was taking too much of a risk, as well as too much of the burden. Lawrence placed the disk he had into the computer at his secretary's desk. After downloading it, he inserted a fresh disk and made a copy.

Once he had finished copying the information, he deleted the downloaded version from the computer. He handed the original copy to Kelly. He knew they would check the disk to ensure it was the original and not a copy.

"Now remember, do exactly what I told you. Don't vary and don't be creative. Do exactly what I told you to do, and everything will work out fine," he said.

He picked up the phone and arranged for a taxi to pick her up in front of the building.

"What are you going to do?" she asked.

"It is better you don't know. Now just follow the plan, and we will be together real soon. You better get going," he said.

She began to turn and walk towards the door when she suddenly stopped. She spun back around and walked back into his waiting arms.

"I love you Peanut, I really do love you," she said.

"Peanut, now that's more like it. I love you too. Now go on, get outta here will you," he said.

She backed up, smiled at him, and turned and walked towards the door. He watched as she opened the door and walked through it.

Conner watched as the taxi bearing Kelly pulled up in front of her brownstone. He watched as she paid the driver and then jogged up the stairs. That was odd, he thought. She was supposed to be home. Perhaps he was slipping in his old age. Did she leave and he didn't see her? He sat in the car for a few moments, and then retrieved his SAT phone and dialed Mike Baker. The line was busy. Another odd coincidence, never before had the phone been busy.

Conner began to question his own paranoia. What did it matter if she was not there when he arrived, and who cared if the phone was busy? He began to feel relief for not actually having made contact with Mike Baker. He was here now, and she was home. In the end, he thought, that was all that mattered. He shifted in the seat and settled in for what remained of his time there. It was early morning, and he wouldn't have to baby-sit much longer.

The first thing Kelly did was to dial the special number Mike had given her in case of any unscheduled events. If any event qualified as an unscheduled one, tonight was definitely it.

"Yes?" came the voice on the other end.

"We have to talk, now!" she replied.

"What's the rush my dear," he said.

"He was here, here in my home. We have to talk," she said.

The phone went silent, only the gentle sound of static air was evident.

"Stay put. I will be there within the hour," he said.

The phone went dead again. Only this time, the dead air had a haunting feel to it. She hoped that Lawrence knew what he was doing. She removed the disk from her purse and began to pace the floor, awaiting the arrival of the man who wanted kill the only man she had ever loved. Too nervous to relax, she paced for 20 minutes.

She heard a car door shut and moved towards the window. She heard another car door shut in the distance and watched as a man approached Mike Baker.

The two men exchanged words, which at times seemed to be heated. After the brief exchange, the other man turned away and walked back up the street. Neither man looked pleased. She watched as Mike Baker turned and made his way towards the stairs to her brownstone. She answered the door before he even had the chance to knock.

"Think it took you long enough?" she said.

"What's this business of him being here?" he asked.

"You should know. I see you had a man watching me," she replied.

"That man is no concern of yours," he replied.

"Excuse me?" she said.

"Enough with the games. Are you going to fill me in on your little unscheduled rendezvous?" he said.

"Something spooked him. I don't know what it was or why, so don't ask. He showed up here in a panic, talking crazy about how they were out to get him. When I asked him who they were, he just kept talking. He said they had killed too many people, and they were trying to kill him because of some information he had. He told me that they had destroyed what he had, but he told me that he had made a copy just in case," she said.

"And?" Mike said.

"And he gave me the copy to keep. He said I was the only one he could trust, and that if anything happened to him, I should see that the Independent Counsel gets the disk," she said.

"And?" Mike said again.

She paused for a moment and looked at him. She attempted to read his demeanor, trying to figure out if she could in fact trust him. But that was not going to happen. He was like a statue, no facial expressions or shifts in body language. She had to gamble and trust that Lawrence knew what he was doing.

"And, before you get the disk I need to hear those magic words," she replied.

"You have my promise that good old Mom and Dad will live out their lives in peace and comfort," he said.

She reached into her pocket and produced the disk, hesitating momentarily before handing it to him.

"I must say that I am extremely pleased. It seems as though my trust in you has been justified. It also seems that our investment in you has been productive," he said.

"What are you going to do to him?" she asked.

"Do you really care?" he replied.

"Oh all right, if you must know. We are going to do nothing. We have what we want."

She knew he was lying, she could see it in his cold eyes, and she could hear it hidden deep in his voice.

"You have done well my dear. I think we may be able to call the slate clean," he said.

"Do you mean that?" she said.

He only smiled at her. Holding the disk up he waved it at her and turned to leave. An evil laughter trailed behind him as he left.

Kelly knew that the only way to be free of him was to destroy him, and that is what she hoped for. She walked to the window and watched as the man re-appeared and spoke briefly with Mike. She watched as he showed the man the disk, and then she watched as he poked his finger in the man's chest, uttering what seemed to be few words.

What Kelly hadn't heard was Mike Baker's order to Conner Braxton to eliminate Lawrence Brazelton at all costs and with extreme prejudice. The man simply nodded, turned, and walked away.

Mike Baker looked up at the window and smiled once again at Kelly before entering his car as the driver shut the door. She hated him. She hated his cocky attitude and smug behavior. More than anything, she wanted to see him go down.

# Chapter - - 20

As dawn broke Lawrence, made his way out of his office building. He walked several blocks before grabbing a taxi and heading to the other side of town to meet with Lucky. If everything had gone as planned, Kelly was safe for now after producing for her employer, and the focus was now centered on locating him. He was comfortable with that because he would soon be leaving town. A move he knew that they couldn't anticipate. He was concerned with the fact that they had come so close to finding him. He was certain that it was a traced phone call that had led them to him, but doubt still lingered.

The stakes were now higher and the spotlight was on him. If they had taken the bait, they would view him as irrational and desperate, entrusting his only security to someone else. They would have orders to kill him on sight. His only comfort was knowing what their plans were and the fact that their view of him was an altered state of reality.

The cab driver pulled up to the Lucky's Rentown lot. Lawrence paid him and gave him a rather sizable tip. He walked through the back gate, which was unlocked. That was a good sign. It meant that Lucky remembered the early meeting time.

"You know, I would only get up this freakin early for my best customer. I hope that you can appreciate that simple fact," Lucky said.

" I do. Believe me I do. Did you get everything that I asked for?" Lawrence asked.

"Whatta ya, kiddin? You some kinda a funny man or what? Of course I got you covered. Now may I ask if you got me covered?" Lucky asked.

"Got you covered," Lawrence said as he tossed a wad of cash to Lucky.

"Nice, very nice. America ain't she beautiful!" Lucky said as he raised the money to his nose and took in a big whiff.

"Anything I should know before I go?" Lawrence asked.

"Well, yea, the car. She's hot. You shouldn't have no trouble. Just don't get pulled over or nothin, if you know what I mean," Lucky said.

"What do you mean I shouldn't have any trouble? And is there anything else you would like to share with the class?" Lawrence said.

"Funny, I like that, share with the class. You're a funny guy. I mean the car they are lookin for looks nothing like the car you see before you. That is unless you get pulled over or somethin, like I said. Besides, whatta ya want on such short notice?" Lucky replied.

"You're right. You did good Lucky. I suppose I don't need to return this one right, no time limits, restrictions, extra charges?" Lawrence said.

"Nah, keep it. Consider it a valued customer bonus," Lucky replied.

"Thanks again Lucky. In some strange way, I am starting to like you. Oh, and if anyone asks…" Lawrence began to say.

"I never seen ya," Lucky said.

Lawrence got into the black Ford Explorer. Somewhere some yuppie is having a fit, he thought. He fastened his seatbelt and watched as Lucky rolled open the gate. He smiled and waved at him as he drove past. In the rear view mirror, he could see Lucky counting the wad of cash he had just received. Lawrence was on his way, and he prayed that this wasn't just another wild goose chase. He was counting on finding something, anything that could help tie this whole mess together.

Conner spent the early morning hours simply driving. He had to cool off before returning to brief the team on its new directives. He was still angry over his confrontation with Mike Baker. He was not sure whether he has angry with Baker or himself. All he knew for sure was that he was pissed. First, for not knowing how close he was to the target. Secondly, because he was not used to such verbal reprimands. What he did know, was that he needed to calm down before he went back.

In some ways his job had been made easier. Assassination alone was no problem. In other ways, it had become more of a

180

challenge. In most cases, you worked with targets that were on a fixed schedule. You learned their daily routine, and you scouted locations for easy access and escape. In this situation, he was dealing with a man who had no schedule, a man who was on the run, and by all accounts scared as hell. Was it impossible? No, it was not. Was it going to be difficult? Yes, but that is the nature of the business. He found himself in a much calmer mood as he approached the warehouse district.

He parked the car and found that much to his amazement, he was late. As he entered the large warehouse, he saw that his team was sitting quietly around the conference table. Each one looked up, and he could see that they wanted to say something.

"I know. I'm late. I don't need to be reminded," he said.

"Our objective has changed. Mr. Brazelton met with his girlfriend last night sometime. She was able to get the remaining copy of the records we needed. Before she could contact anyone, he left. According to her, he is in a state of extreme paranoia and is acting irrationally," he said.

"So where does that leave us?" Carlos asked.

"We have the task of locating him and putting a bullet in his head. It is as simple as that," replied Conner.

"Simple!" exclaimed Victor.

"I am aware of your concerns as to the ease of locating and eliminating the target. We do have several advantages in this particular situation. He is not a pro. We are. He is scared, and he is no longer in possession of any leverage. He will make a mistake, and we will capitalize on that mistake. I want you to break up your teams of two and hit the streets. It is a big city, and he can't hide for long. We know where he is not, so lets hit where he may be. We have defined some of his behaviors, so lets exploit them and find him. When he is found, and we will find him, I want him eliminated. No questions, no hesitation. Am I clear?" he said.

Conner looked at each man and was greeted with a simple nod. Each man then got up and went about preparing to hit the streets. They each carried a small briefcase that contained the tools of their trade. As usual, Jason Wheeler would remain behind and work his magic via his computer, his particular tool of choice.

Conner acknowledged the men and walked to his office. He had not slept in over 24 hours, and he struggled with the need for sleep and the need to finish the job. He chose to rest. Shutting his door, he turned of the light and lay on the small cot in the corner of the room.

Lawrence had made it safely out of town and was now making his way towards Clay's mountain retreat. He had a map opened on the passenger's seat and had decided to take the back roads to his destination. It would add about 2 additional hours to the journey, but he figured that it was better to be safe than to be caught.

He found the drive to be rather peaceful. His thoughts were generally warm, and he reflected on his relationship with Kelly. He knew they would have some issues to work out when this was over, but he felt only warmth in his heart for her. He realized that he could very easily have brushed her aside and discounted her loyalty. She had, after all, been less than honest with him. He knew after watching her in that small, dirty room and listening to her, that she loved him. That she cared for him as much as he cared for her. Maybe his judgement had been clouded by that love.

At this point, none of that truly mattered. He was focused on the finish line. He was anxious to see this through, to get to the point where he could answer those questions. He was feeling somewhat like a kid in high school, in love for the first time. He liked that feeling, and he hoped the excitement would never cease.

Mike Baker was full of himself. His confidence in the Brazelton affair had been bolstered by the acquisition of the final pieces of the information puzzle. As he sat in his office, his thoughts drifted to the need to have Lawrence gone. He realized that Lawrence was no longer a legitimate threat, but more of a nuisance now. Without the documentation showing the President's involvement, he was just a man with a story. Mike's confidence began to level off and return to earth. He knew that the Independent Counsel would still be interested in the story, even without documentation.

Mike began to realize the urgency in the elimination of Lawrence Brazelton. His confidence in the Dogwatch was in question, due to the events of last night. He began to question their ability to see that the problem was handled. As his mind worked through the possible ways to hasten the elimination of Lawrence, he was hit with a stunning idea.

Mike Baker was about to do something that hadn't been done in years. He was about to call an emergency meeting of the Group, in its entirety. If this idea was going to work, he would need not only the blessings of the others, he would need their resources as well.

As evening approached and the sun began to set, Lawrence found himself in the small community of Valmont. Clay Danvers cabin was only another 30 minutes from the small trading post he had stopped at. The small town of Valmont was old. Most of its residents knew each other well, and the use of last names was entirely unnecessary. Visitors to this small community were rare.

Most of the property in this tight knit community had been in families for generations. The fishing was excellent, and that did account for the occasional angler passing through to test their luck.

Lawrence walked into the small trading post and made his way towards the cooler that was at the side of the register. He listened to the proprietor and several locals as they spoke about the recent events that had created some excitement. As the conversation progressed, he noted that it was devoted to the death of his friend, as well as the fact that the small town had been besieged by several-unmarked black Suburban's. The men went back and forth regarding the identity of the visitors. One man called them "Shadow Men," while the others just referred to them as Feds and suits.

After retrieving a bottled water from the cooler, he made his way to a rack directly behind the men who were having the discussion. He continued to shop and listen. They talked about the time that the men had spent at the old Danvers place and the fact that each one of them had been question extensively. They were asked about the frequency of visits by Danvers to the small community and his activities while he was there.

Each man had a theory and Lawrence listened intensely. When he figured he had heard enough, he walked to the register with his goods and laid them on the counter. The same men who had paid little attention to him when he entered, were now looking him over form head to toe and were now silent. The proprietor finally broke the silence.

"Anything else?"

"That will do it," Lawrence replied.

"So, what brings ya here Young Fella?" the owner said as he punched the buttons on the antique register.

"Just passing through. Thought I might maybe fish a little," Lawrence replied.

"It's a little late in the season for fishing. That will be $7.56," the man said.

Lawrence paid the man and gathered up his purchase. The men continued their silence and watched as Lawrence walked out the door.

"Smooth, you're real smooth Lawrence," he said to himself.

He climbed into the Explorer and opened the water. After taking a sizable drink, he started the car and drove off. As he drove, he wondered if the men in the black Suburban's were still around. Instead of driving directly to the cabin, he decided to tour the country and make sure that the "Shadow Men" were indeed gone.

After two hours of driving every back road and dirt road he crossed, he now found himself driving down a small dirt road that lead to the Danvers cabin. He pulled off the road and drove into the trees about a half-mile from the Cabin. He had visited the cabin once with Danvers, but that was a long time ago. Opening the back of the Explorer, he retrieved several of the items that Lucky had gotten for him. He pulled the .45 from his backpack, chambered a round, and then placed the gun in his waistband. After throwing the backpack over his shoulder, he picked up a pair of night vision goggles.

It was a cloudy evening and with the sun down, the moon offered no assistance by providing any light. He put the goggles on and hit the switch above his right ear. As the goggles powered up, he could hear a faint whine that was followed by a soft flash, and then his world turned green. It took him a moment to compensate for the new form of vision. After a few seconds, his balance and sense of direction returned, and he began the short walk to his destination. Anticipation built with each step. What would he find? Would he be alone, or would he have company? His heart rate was increasing with each step. He had reached the end of the trees and crouched down low as he surveyed his target.

The cabin was dark and no vehicles or movement were present. He looked past the cabin to the lake. It was calm and void of any craft or persons. He removed the backpack and retrieved the photograph. He had made marks on the photo indicating the north and south ends of the small building. He turned the picture to reflect its position in relevance to the cabin in front of him. He found what he thought was the area. He returned the photo to his backpack. Just like he had seen in the movies, he made his way towards the cabin, quick and low. He reached the spot, and he hoped that it was the location Clay had intended him to find.

He began first by digging around in the dirt at the foot of the cabin. After working that area with no success, he began to look at the actual structure. It was a log cabin constructed out of large pine logs. He moved his hands over each log hoping to find something. He slowly worked his way from the base of the cabin to as high as he could reach, but he found nothing.

Figuring that maybe what he was looking for was actually inside, he kicked the bottom log in frustration. It sounded hollow. He dropped to his knees and removed the .45 from his waist and began to tap on the log. He then tapped the log above it, and it was solid. He tapped the bottom log again, and to his amazement, it did sound hollow. He placed the .45 back in his waist and began a much closer exam of the bottom log. He

185

looked for any possible access to the inside of the log, but it wasn't until he twisted it, that he discovered its secret.

Once he had removed the cap covering the log, he eagerly reached inside. Brushing past cobwebs and dust, he removed a plastic trash bag and opened it. Inside, he discovered several journals. He quickly placed them back in the bag and looked around, as if he expected to see something or someone. He wanted to see what the journals contained right then and there. Instead, he gathered his senses and placed the cap back on the log and quickly made his way back to his vehicle. He threw his backpack into the car, as well as the goggles, but he kept the .45 tucked in his waistband. He placed the trash bag on the seat next to him and started the car.

As he drove down the back roads of Valmont, he continued to glance at the bag on the seat. It was calling him, asking him to stop and look. He had to fight the urge to stop and read the journals Clay had led him to. He had to find a safe place to do that. He had passed a small travel lodge about 60 miles outside of Valmont, and he figured he would get a room. Then he would have plenty of time to read. He drove on and continued to glance at the bag, wondering what secrets were contained in its pages and what role those secrets played in the death of Clay Danvers.

Old Sam watched as the parade of vehicles entered the garage. He recognized each of the vehicles, except for the last one to arrive. The two men in the front seat were well dressed and very serious looking. They eyed the old security guard as they passed, as if to tell him that they meant business. Sam watched as the car slowly passed him. The rear windows of the Cadillac Limousine were pitch dark, and the occupants were safe in their anonymity. Sam had been notified of the arrivals and was instructed to let them pass without the usual stops for identity verification.

Mike Baker stood at the doorway to the meeting room used by the Group. He greeted each man as they entered the room with a handshake. The last to arrive was a rather irritated Preston Wesley.

"I hope you have a good reason for this little gathering," the President said.

"Indeed I do Sir," replied Mike.

"Well, it better be. You have no idea how much I hate those damn tunnels and all the shit that's involved with me leaving for this type of get together," the President said.

"I fully understand. However, it was unavoidable and very necessary" Mike replied.

The newest member of the Group, Chase Walters, followed the President. He appeared to be the most uncomfortable of all the attendees of the meeting. After each of the members had had a chance to acknowledge one another, Mike Baker motioned for everyone to have a seat.

"First, let me take a moment to thank each of you for responding to my invitation. I realize that this is somewhat of an unprecedented meeting. Generally, our business is conducted without the need for face-to-face meetings. Over the past several weeks, we have been in a race with the Independent Counsel to thwart the addition of further information to his campaign against our President."

"Today, we are one step closer to winning that race. As you all are aware, the Independent Counsel had a meeting recently with Lawrence Brazelton. While this seemed to be somewhat of a nuisance rather than a problem, we soon discovered that it was indeed a problem," Mike paused.

"And why is that? I was under the impression that Brazelton had been handled long ago," said the President.

"So did we all Sir. We learned that he had copies of all the original documentation pertaining to your involvement with the Cordona family. We also learned that this was the substance of his meeting with the Independent Counsel. Had you been more forthcoming in the beginning, we might have been able to avoid this all together," Mike said.

"I don't have to explain myself to you. What I want to know, is why now, after all these years? I thought we had bought his silence and his loyalty," the President said.

"Love, I expect," replied Mike.

"Love! What kind of answer is that? I need something better than love, damn it!" shouted the President.

Mike did not acknowledge the somewhat childish outburst from the President. He simply looked at him as a mother would look at a child who was out of line. The President seemed somewhat shocked by the parental gaze of his keeper and fell silent.

"And the information?" asked Chase Walters.

"Gone. We were able to locate it and destroy it. And before you ask, we know that we have not only destroyed it, we also have obtained any copies as well," Mike said.

"Then what is the purpose of this meeting? If the threat has been eliminated, then why is there a need for us to meet? Considering how risky this type of meeting is, and given the fact that if what you say is true, then Brazelton has nothing," Neil Reyna said.

"Nothing? He has a story to tell. And each of you is aware of how eager the media, the people, and especially the Independent Counsel are to hear a good story," Mike said.

He paused and turned to face the window. It was a dramatic pause, intentionally done in preparation for the disclosure of his plan to eliminate Lawrence as a threat. He began to speak again.

"Gentlemen, we are on the verge of a new century. Our President has completed two very successful terms in office and has assisted each of us in our endeavors. This administration is on the verge of turning the reigns over to an administration that would enable us to continue our pursuits. The Vice President will win the next election, and our newest member will retain his post, thus ensuring our agenda and continued prosperity. If this threat were to go public at this juncture, it would cast a cloud over this administration and thus jeopardize the integrity of this organization. This we can not tolerate."

"Again, why the need for this meeting. You have handled situations like this in the past. Why do you need us? Just kill the son of a bitch," Patrick Cortina said.

"We don't know where he is," replied Mike Baker.

"What? You don't know where he is?" shouted the President.

188

"It is a large city, and a man can get lost if he so chooses," replied Mike Baker.

"Ok, enough. What are you proposing we do then?" asked Patrick.

"I am so glad you asked."

"Lawrence Brazelton was a former partner in a law firm that came under fire. Ultimately, he left the firm in disgrace. Since that time, his wife has died, his son has died, and he no longer has the respect that he worked so hard to obtain..." Mike was saying when he was interrupted.

"Get to the point. Where is this going?" the President said as his confidence was again surfacing.

"If we are to find the man, we need more eyes than my team has. I propose we implicate Brazelton in the death of Clay Danvers. We can place him as the last person to see Danvers alive. We can establish a motive, revenge. He killed Danvers to pay back the President whom he blames for his losses. We can establish a direct threat to the President himself. Making this a matter of National Security. With every Law enforcement agency looking for him, we can have him in custody in no time. Then we can deal with him on our own," Mike said.

The room fell silent as each member of the Group contemplated the feasibility of the scenario Mike had proposed.

"But what about the Independent Counsel? Won't it seem rather odd that the man he is interested in winds up killing Danvers and threatening the President?" asked Neil Reyna.

"Our sources within the Justice Department have confirmed that the initial meeting between Brazelton and Justin was preliminary. No details or information was exchanged. It was basically a "what if meeting"," Mike said.

"That still doesn't mean that Justin is going to back down. I think it will serve to peak his interests. That son of a bitch has a hard on for me," said the President.

"Maybe so, but without Brazelton, without what Brazelton was going to give him, he will still be chasing his tail and making himself look like a complete ass. Our spin on this whole Independent Counsel fiasco has worked to perfection to this point. The public looks at Paul Justin like a rabid dog. Without physical evidence, he is viewed as the other party's lap dog, out to take down a popular President. The Independent Counsel statute is up this year, and the public is sick of the abuse. Trust me. This will work," said Mike.

The Group seemed to be in agreement. Each one nodded their approval of the new directive. Bart Sullivan would see that the media at large would begin their smear campaign on Lawrence Brazelton. Labeling him as a mad man, responsible for the death of Clay Danvers and a threat to the President himself.

Chase Walters would work on the inside with the Justice Department, coordinating the law enforcement end of things, as well as run interference against the Independent Counsel. The others would work with their contacts. Lawrence Brazelton's life was about to be turned inside out, as well as upside down.

With the direction set, the meeting ended. Once again, Mike Baker sat in his opulent surroundings, looking forward to a continued life of excess, a life that had been temporarily interrupted by an annoying little man. A man who had no concept of the level of power he was challenging.

# Chapter - - 21

Lawrence sat at the small table in his modest motel room. He had just begun to read the journals left behind by Clay Danvers. He was unaware that his life was being altered and that others were planning to change the course of his destiny. He read with a mixture of horror and amazement. Clay Danvers had written his life story in the pages of the seven journals that Lawrence had recovered.

As Lawrence read the contents of the journals, he realized that the information he had kept and struggled to maintain, paled by comparison. Over the course of the evening, he read in detail about the rise of the current President. His destiny was set into motion as early as his senior year in college. Lawrence learned that his arrival at the law firm of Stoner, Winston & Kaplan was by greater design. That is where his political career had begun and for good reason.

He read about the momentum of a political machine and how it crushed whatever stood in its way. There were detailed accounts of cover-ups, bribes, and intimidation. He even read about the meetings that were held in reference to his own fate.

Clay had chronicled all of the events that had occurred in the making of a President, from the men behind the scenes, to the real policy makers. He finally figured out the significance of the photograph with the cryptic quote written in red, "You can change the golden rule". Clay had been a member of what he referred to in the journals as simply "The Group". This Group was comprised of several of this nation's wealthiest and most influential men. Their sole purpose was the acquisition of wealth and power.

They had no party affiliations and no aspirations for a New World order. They were not politicians. They were simply capitalists, and they craved power and money. They had an extensive history of obtaining that which they desired through any means necessary. It was accomplished by utilizing the aforementioned tactics of bribery, intimidation, and the corruption of individuals to further their agenda. These men embodied the golden rule and they believed in its promise. They had taken it seriously and pursued it ravenously.

Lawrence closed the last journal as the sun began to build and break through the flimsy curtains of his room. He was filled with several emotions, fear, depression, regret, and desperation. Who could he trust? He now knew whom he couldn't trust. Clay had provided him with a detailed list of corrupt individuals and their despicable activities. He began to realize the significance of the information he possessed.

What had begun as a journey to expose one man as a fraud and a liar, had snowballed into a scandal that threatened a nation. The repercussions would be vast, and the scars would be deep and long lasting. Lawrence contemplated his actions. He thought about just burning the journals and exposing the President using the information he had on his activities at the law firm. But that became unacceptable when he realized that the men behind the President deserved to be exposed and punished. As he worked it through in his mind, he realized that the only way to be truly free was to take them all down, with swift and precise determination.

Kelly had not slept well at all. She spent the past day and night pacing about, wondering if Lawrence was safe. Frustrated with the fact she could do nothing, she walked towards the coffee table and picked up the television remote control. Maybe some TV would take her away from her present thoughts. A picture of Lawrence instantly greeted her, and the caption below it read, "Breaking News." She fumbled for the remote that she had tossed onto the couch and quickly turned up the volume.

*"At this hour, his whereabouts are unknown. If you have any information that may lead authorities to his whereabouts, you are asked to call the 800 number on you screen. He is considered armed and extremely dangerous…"*

Kelly watched and listened in disbelief. The newsman moved onto another story. She began switching to the other channels for more details. She spent the better part of the next two hours listening to varied accounts of the search for Lawrence Brazelton. The general consensus was that he was being sought in connection to the death of Clay Danvers and an apparent threat on the life of the President. He was considered armed and dangerous and was operating in a diminished capacity. She wanted to turn the television off, but chose instead to leave it on with the volume down. All she could do was wait in a state of disbelief. Visions of some hero cop blowing Lawrence away played on in her mind. She had no way to contact him and no way to assist him.

She had given the disk to Mike Baker as Lawrence had instructed her to do, and therefore, she didn't even have that if something happened to him. Her nerves began to settle somewhat as she realized all she could do was pray and hope that Lawrence knew what he was doing, and more importantly who he was dealing with.


The President had just finished his weekly cabinet meeting and was now in the privacy of the Oval Office. His lone companion was Chase Walters. They had just finished watching the newest news bulletin on GNN.

"How did I ever get so deep into this?" the President asked.

"Lawrence was a friend for crying out loud. He took me under his wing at the firm. Shit, I even ate dinner with his family!" he continued.

"Mr. President, we can't undo what is already done," Chase replied.

"You fit right in don't you?" the President said.

"I am a realist Mr. President, and as such, I understand that the decisions we make are rooted in a much larger picture than we realize at times. What would you rather have happen? Would you prefer that your past, as well as the alliances you have formed, be exposed? That history looks at you in disgrace rather than triumph? I ask you, what would you like to do?" Chase said.

"I wish it would all just go away," the President said.

"And it will. Things have always taken care of themselves. You are a great man Sir, and you are destined for a vaunted place in history. You have a tremendous legacy and the world will remember Preston A. Wesley as a great President," Chase said.

"Will they?" said the President.

"Please leave me, and see that I am not disturbed," he said.

"Yes Mr. President," Chase said as he turned and walked to the door.

There he stood. He was most powerful, the most influential man in the free world. Yet, for some reason, he felt like a prisoner of that world rather than its leader. Over the years, he had successfully limited his contact and involvement with the Group. Now he was up to his elbows in it. He realized that Chase Walters was right. He knew that you had to break a few eggs to make an omelet. He had to look at it that way. He had to rationalize it away. For some reason, he couldn't do that this time. His heart was heavy and mind was numb. Numb with the knowledge that he was party to yet another man's destruction.

The Dogwatch was gathered at the warehouse. Their instructions were simple. Once Lawrence was located, they would move in and take him out. Jason Wheeler had every newscast plastered across several monitors and was monitoring every law enforcement transmission as well. He had tapped the special 800 number being used to tip off the authorities in the event of a sighting.

It was a waiting game, and it was what they had grown accustomed to. Conner had not been shy about his displeasure at the course this assignment had taken. He knew that the risks were terrible in this type of situation. Risks he was not happy about putting his team in the middle of. If they could get to the target before the law, then they could take him out. If the law got there first the job would move to another level. His mind drifted towards the infamous footage of Jack Ruby shooting Lee Harvey Oswald when he was in custody. They were facing the possibility of having to do just that. So, he too sat and waited.

Lawrence heard the newspaper hit the front door of his motel room. It was the one luxury the motel provided its guests. He opened the door and picked up the paper. What he saw sent him into what he believed was a cardiac arrest. There on the front page was a picture of him. It was a current photograph and appeared to be from some sort of security camera. It was a bit fuzzy, but recent. He was still wearing the same hat as in the picture as well as the same jacket. Next to it was a better picture of him. It looked like the one on his driver's license. He looked around the parking lot to make sure no one had seen him, and then he quickly shut the door and began to read the accompanying article.

According to the article, he was wanted in connection with the mysterious death of Clay Danvers. He was considered unstable and dangerous.

"Unstable? Dangerous?" he said out loud, which was followed by laughter.

He knew that they were out to get him, but this, this bordered on comical. He realized that these events would make his task that much harder, but he couldn't help but find just a little humor in it. He looked at the journals on the table and thought to himself, if you want unstable, I'll show you unstable.

He gathered up the journals and placed them in his backpack. He walked out of his room and directly to the Ford Explorer. He climbed in and shut the door, noting that he would have to thank Lucky some day for the dark tint on the windows.

He sat in the Explorer and realized he was a hunted man, in a stolen car purchased from a Mafia wannabe in possession of information that could topple the government. Taken one at a time, it could be viewed as an everyday occurrence. Put them together and he thought about the fact that he had the makings of a best selling novel.

It was back to the city, and back to his new pal Lucky. He needed help, and Lucky was the only friend he had. Lawrence had several things going for him. He knew everything they did. He knew the identity of all the players, and the only information they had was what he had given Kelly.

The light at the end of the tunnel was in the form of Paul Justin. All he needed to do was get to him, and the rest would be academic. He knew it wasn't going to be easy, but at least this time the odds were in his favor.

Mike Baker's frustration was growing. He had hoped that the release of Lawrence's picture and the intense media blitz would have produced results by now. He sat in his office and watched the same broadcasts as everyone else, listened to the same law enforcement transmissions, and had access to the 800-tip line.

His frustration level came down a notch as he listened to a call from a gentleman in Valmont, Virginia. He claimed that he had seen the man in the paper and on the TV just yesterday. He recounted how the man milled around his trading post, then bought some water, a bag of pretzels, and some other items. The operator on the call was one of many off duty officers brought in to handle calls. He questioned the man at great length.

He hadn't seen what the man was driving, and other than recognizing him, that was about all he could offer. The officer thanked the man for his call and told him that local law enforcement, and possibly Federal officials, would be out to take a statement. Mike knew that the Dogwatch was listening to the same conversation.

"Valmont?" Mike said out loud as he stared at the ceiling.

He wondered why the name sounded so familiar and wanted to know why he should recognize it. His frustration returned, as the word Valmont trickled out of his mouth in succession like drops from a leaking faucet. He picked up his phone and dialed.

"Yes?" Conner said.

"The son of a bitch is at Danvers cabin. It is just outside of Valmont!" Mike barked into the phone.

"Got it," Conner said and terminated the call.

Mike's confidence was at an all time high. Lawrence was probably attempting to hide out in or around Danvers cabin. The boys would take a chopper to Valmont and be there before the locals or even the Feds figured it out. Then, and only then, would Lawrence Brazelton simply be just a memory.

The drive back to the city was long, boring, and rather uneventful. Lawrence had had visions of massive roadblocks, vehicle searches, and the like. Instead, he got clear sailing for the better part of his journey. Once he hit DC, his nerves became a little more sensitive. In the close quarters of the rush hour traffic, he swore he could feel the eyes of every motorist as they pierced through the tinted windows.

With each honk of another car's horn, his reaction grew more dramatic. He felt like simply parking the car and walking, but that was out of the question. He continued to maneuver the streets and slowly made his way to the Lucky's Rentown lot. It was rush hour and the drive was tedious. He pulled into the lot and drove to the gate at the rear. He honked his horn one time and waited.

After a few seconds, Lucky came out from behind the gate. He stood and stared at Lawrence for a moment. Lawrence could tell that he was thinking whether or not it was a good idea to have any further involvement with him. Good thing for Lawrence that Lucky was a man who liked money, was curious by nature, and hated the government. He opened the gate and motioned for Lawrence to pull through. Lawrence got out of the car, and before he could say thank you, Lucky was in his face.

"Is it true what they are sayin about you?"

"Did you do that guy or what?" he continued.

"I mean if your crazy, I think I should know that from you. I think you owe me that, us bein so close and all" Lucky said.

"No. I didn't do that guy to use your vernacular, and no I am not crazy," replied Lawrence.

"I didn't think so, but I hadda hear it from you," Lucky said.

"I need your help Lucky. I need to clear my name and get the men responsible for all of this. Will you help me?" asked Lawrence.

"I think I can do that," replied Lucky after a momentary pause.

"Good. Do you have a place I can work?" Lawrence said.

"Sure, follow me," replied Lucky.

Lawrence grabbed his backpack from the Explorer, as well as the laptop he had picked up with the Explorer. Lucky led him to an old mobile home at the rear of the lot. Outside it looked like scrap, inside was a different story. It had been converted into a rather nice office. He figured that Lucky did some of his questionable business from within these walls, but that didn't bother him in the slightest.

"Is this ok?" asked Lucky.

"Just fine. Do I have an outside line here?" asked Lawrence.

"Yeah, the phone is on the desk," replied Lucky.

Lawrence thanked Lucky, as he left him to do his business. He sat behind the desk and set up the laptop. He removed the disk he had copied form the backpack. After he connected the phone line to the small black box he always carried, he connected the pigtail to the laptop. The black box scrambled his connection to the Internet, making it difficult to trace the origin. He booted up the computer and inserted the copied disk. He wanted to make sure the information was intact.

Paul Justin sat in the confines of his office and alternated between televised versions of breaking news on Lawrence Brazelton, as well as scanning the print accounts of the situation. He knew that the allegations were bullshit. He also knew that the media at large had increased its efforts to discredit his probe into the affairs of Preston A. Wesley.

His reputation as an impartial and dedicated jurist had suffered devastating blows over the past year. He had developed information that pointed to the President's involvement in numerous unsavory activities during his personal life and political career. The information he had garnered only proved to provide a link, a thread of possible involvement. Each time he had come close to substantiating his suspicions, the rug was pulled out from under him, and he was left with what amounted to circumstantial evidence. With a President who was experiencing the highest approval ratings in history, you needed more than circumstantial evidence.

This time was no different than times past. He had a promising witness in Lawrence Brazelton, but once again, he found himself flat on his ass. In the end, he was looking up at a President who was laughing, as he held the rug that was the foundation of any hope he had to finally nail him.

Paul Justin watched and read and realized that with the Independent Counsel statute approaching its end, and a public who had been manipulated by a compliant media, he was finished. He didn't know what Lawrence had to offer. Their one and only meeting revolved around preliminary discussions and the setting of some guidelines for future meetings. He had made certain assurances to Lawrence. He had promised him that he would only have to deal with him. He had given Lawrence his personal pager number for contact in the future.

Paul Justin's hope for any deal with Lawrence Brazelton was dwindling by the minute. He had not heard from him since their initial meeting, and considering the events that were unfolding before him the likelihood of any future meeting was fading. The President would be vindicated. He personally would be vilified, and Lawrence Brazelton, well, that chapter was yet to be written. But he knew the outcome would, more than likely, be tragic.

He turned the television off and cleared his desk of the articles that proved more to taunt him, rather than lift him. The office was quiet and he reclined back in his chair and contemplated his now bleak future. As he sat in his chair and reflected on the life that he had worked so hard to maintain. Then, he felt his pager vibrate against his side. It surprised him just a little, and he reached back and removed it from its place on his belt. He looked at the display, and to his shock and amazement, the first three digits were the ones he had given Lawrence as a code for future communication.

"I'll be, Lazarus lives!" he shouted.

He read the numbers following the three-digit code and quickly picked up his phone and dialed. He paused and thought better of using the phone in his office. He quickly grabbed his jacket and bolted out the door. He hit the lobby running and slowed down his pace, as to not draw attention to himself. He knew that he was always under the watchful eye of the media, as well as the cronies of the President. As he approached the front door, he witnessed the typical gathering of the media and decided it might be better to leave via the garage. He did a 180 and walked towards the garage. His heart raced in anticipation of hearing from Lawrence.

Lawrence had spent the past two hours on the Internet. He had pulled up maps of the city and was scouting locations for the next step in his plan. He had spent some of his time creating a little offering to Paul Justin. He removed a disk from his laptop. It contained selected records from his original documentation regarding Wesley's time at the firm, as well as some accounts and names from the Danvers journals. The names were critical, because they would provide Justin with the players within his own investigative teams that had been compromised.

The information he had provided was just enough to tease the Independent Counsel and peak his curiosity. He also had included several demands that must be met prior to any meeting or the release of the balance of the information.

Lawrence had just paged Paul Justin and was waiting for the return call. He hoped that Justin would not only return his call, but that he would be smart about doing it.

As he sat and waited, he realized that he was in a state of peace. He felt in control for the first time, and his world seemed to be settling. The phone interrupted his reflections.

"Are you alone?" Lawrence asked.

"Yes I'm alone. I am in the damn guard shack in the parking garage," replied Justin.

"Good, I want you to listen. I want you to go Tyson's Mall just outside of Georgetown. In the men's clothing department of Nordstrom you will see a man looking at sport coats. He will know who you are. I want you to take the jacket he places back on the rack when you make eye contact. When you get into the dressing room you will find a disk in the right inside pocket. Make sure and be there by 8:30. I will contact you after that," Lawrence said.

He didn't wait for a response. He simply hung the phone up. Phase one of his plan was now complete. Lucky was standing there watching and listening as Lawrence made the call.

"Are you sure you want to do this?" asked Lawrence.

"Sure, kinda makes me feel like a secret agent and all," replied Lucky.

"Are you sure you know the face?" Lawrence said as he motioned for Lucky to look at the picture on the laptop screen once again.

"Yeah, I got the mug," Lucky replied.

"Remember, eye contact, no words. Just make sure he sees you, and then get out of there, understand?"

"Loud and clear."

"All right. Now get out of here."

"Oh, and by the way, thanks. Believe me, I am going to make all of this worth your while my friend."

"And I am going to hold you to that," Lucky replied as he turned to leave.

Lawrence watched as Lucky walked out the door. He turned the laptop back around and looked at the picture of Paul Justin he had downloaded from the Internet. Don't let me down you stubborn prick, he thought, as he looked at the face of the only man he could trust.

# Chapter - - 22

The Dogwatch team had descended on the small community of Valmont and more specifically, the former retreat of Clay Danvers like a bird of prey, literally.  As the team exited the chopper like the well-trained soldiers they were, Conner watched from the comfort of their warehouse command center.  The team members were equipped with a small camera and microphone set attached to their helmets.

As the men approached the cabin with speed and silence, Conner hoped for a quick and lethal ending to this assignment.  No vehicle was present, and they quickly made their way to the cabin, alternating as they advanced, weapons ready to fire.

Each man positioned himself at a corner of the structure and alternated at peering through the windows.  Then with precise timing, they broke simultaneously through the rear door and the front door.  After an extensive room-to-room search, Conner's desired ending was not realized.  He ordered the men to conduct a search of the area for any signs that could lead them to Brazelton.  After that, he ordered them to return to base.  Neither he nor Mike Baker was pleased that the tip had led them to a dead end.

Lucky followed the route to Tyson's Mall in Georgetown that Lawrence had given to him.  He wasn't sure why Lawrence had been so adamant about following his instructions, but Lucky humored him anyway.  He checked his rear view mirror and glanced occasionally at the maps Lawrence had printed out.

He parked his vehicle and checked his watch.  He still had 15 minutes to get to Nordstrom.  Once inside the large department store, he made his way past the perfume snipers and went directly to the men's clothing department.  He located the section that displayed the suits and sports coat selection.  He positioned himself in front of a rack and began to browse.  He tried to look inconspicuous, but was failing.  An older man with and English accent approached.

"That would look dashing on you!" he exclaimed.

"Beat it will ya. I'm just looking, ya limy freak," Lucky said.

The man was offended and walked off in a huff. Lucky spent the next several minutes looking at coats and looking at the other customers as they browsed. Then he saw his pigeon. He slipped the disk into the jacket he was looking at and removed it from the rack. He watched the man casually look at each individual in the clothing department. Their eyes met, and each one knew what was next. Lucky placed the coat back on the rack and walked around to the other side looking at jackets along the way.

Paul Justin approached the jacket that Lucky had replaced and retrieved it. He walked towards the dressing rooms. Lucky had since made his way back to the entrance and was out of the store at about the same time that Paul Justin was removing the disk from the jacket pocket.

The information Paul Justin had received had done its job. It was not enough to prove guilt, but it was an indication that the balance could prove to be devastating. Justin knew that Lawrence could provide him with information pertaining to Wesley's tenure at the firm, but the additional promise of information contained in the journals of Clay Danvers pointed to a much larger conspiracy.

The fact that Lawrence had provided him with names of people on his own investigative team who had been compromised, showed the detail of information contained in the journals. Lawrence indicated that the information in his possession not only implicated the President, but many government officials, as well as members of the private sector, in everything from treason, bribery, and extortion to even murder.

The gravity of the situation began to weigh on Justin's heart. If this information proved to be true and could be substantiated, it could mean the indictments of not just a President, but also many other high-ranking officials. It had begun as the search for the truth about one man's life and his choices. It was now a painful reminder of the true consequences behind the pursuit of power.

Anxious to have unfettered access to the bulk of the information, Paul Justin began making the arrangements to meet the demands specified by Lawrence. The demands were substantial, but Paul Justin knew that if he was going after the President, he needed what Lawrence had. He would answer to Congress later regarding the payment he was about to make. He knew that if the investigation were to result in the convening of impeachment proceedings, the money he was about to spend would not be the central issue.

Lawrence was lying on the couch in the makeshift office when Lucky returned from his little adventure. If Justin agreed to his stipulations, it meant that Lucky would profit greatly for assisting Lawrence and his country. He thought it was interesting that a man like Lucky, who had lived a life of crime, was one of the only people he had been able to trust and rely on. Life was funny that way, he thought.

"Any problems?" he asked.

"Nope, went just like you said it would," Lucky replied.

"Well my friend, all we have to do now is wait. Give the man time to make some choices," Lawrence said.

"You need anything else," Lucky asked.

"Just some peace and quiet," replied Lawrence.

Lucky took his cue and left Lawrence alone. As he lay on the couch, he hoped that Justin could pull the necessary strings and make things happen. He closed his eyes and tried to sleep. He had told Justin he would contact him at noon the following day.

Paul Justin's first move was to contact Kenneth Jeffreye, the Director of the FBI. Before he made any moves, he would have to clean house and do it in a manner that would ensure secrecy. The Director's name did not appear on the list that Lawrence had provided him, so Justin counted on his assistance.

The round up went according to plan. In the early morning hours, the FBI simultaneously arrested the compromised members of the Independent Counsel's team. Additionally, they detained the immediate family of those taken into custody. With his team now free from leaks, he had Kelly Ford picked up, as well as her parents. They were taken to Andrews Air Force Base and held under guard for their own safety and protection. He made arrangements with the Federal Marshals to enter Mr. and Mrs. Ford into the witness protection program. He had his plane fueled and ready for takeoff with no flight plan filed.

Inside the plane was a briefcase containing $100,000.00 and a slip of paper indicating that an additional $2,000,000.00 had been transferred to the offshore account specified by Lawrence. Paul Justin sat in his office with the final stipulation on his desk, $100,000.00 in small denominations. He wasn't sure what it was for. He held his pager in his hand and waited for it to go off.

Mike Baker was furious. The trip to Valmont was a goose egg. They had nothing. No tips were coming in, and no sightings had been reported. Lawrence Brazelton was a ghost. Bart Sullivan had seen to it that the Brazelton story was a non-stop affair. Every other major news outlet had picked it up as well.

Things began to feel out of control, and Mike could feel the situation slipping away from him. He was in a position that was foreign to him. He chastised himself for not eliminating Lawrence in the beginning, and for letting the pity of a weak man like Preston A. Wesley dictate his decision. His fear turned to anger, and his anger clouded any judgement that might have remained. Mike Baker was spiraling downward into a state of advanced diminished capacity. Kill them all, he thought. Kill them all, and let God sort them out.

Lawrence dialed the pager number for Paul Justin. The return call came almost immediately, as Justin had installed a secure line.

"Do we have a deal?" asked Lawrence.

"Yes, everything you have requested has been carried out," replied Justin.

"Kelly?" Lawrence said.

"Safe with her parents at Andrews AFB," Justin replied.

Lawrence felt the last weight lift from his chest. All he ever cared about was Kelly. He had started this whole nasty ordeal to ensure a life with her. Maybe that was going to be the case after all.

"It's your turn. When do I get what I want?" asked Justin.

Lawrence had spent the morning carefully scanning the pages of Clay Danvers journals into his computer. He was not going to turn over the actual journals, rather a very nice detailed version via electronic mail. Coupled with the documentation he had on Wesley's activities at the firm and the contents of the journals, Paul Justin would take down an administration, as well as the people behind it.

He would keep the originals, for much the same reason he had kept the original documentation from the firm, as insurance. Only this time he wouldn't make the same mistake. The journals would remain with him until he could secure them in a safety deposit box, where they would remain until he was certain it was over.

"You will be visited by the same man you saw when you retrieved the disk. You will give him the package containing the $100,000.00, which he will be expecting. You will then be given the information necessary to access the information you desire. Please have your plane land at the airstrip in Falls Church. Once I am on board with Kelly, I will contact him to pay you that visit," Lawrence said.

"How do I know you will keep up your end? And besides, what if I need you to testify?" Justin said.

"Trust me, I have no love for the men you are pursuing. With the information I am giving you, my testimony will be of little use or consequence. You are going to be busy for years to come," Lawrence said.

"I could have you picked up and detained."

"Yes, you could, but then you wouldn't get what you really want. The Presidents head, served on a silver platter. You're wasting time," Lawrence said as he ended the conversation.

Setting the cellular phone on the seat next to him, he looked into the afternoon sky and waited. Waited to be with Kelly and for the nightmare to be over.

Chase Walters could feel something in the air. He had expected to hear from the office of the Independent Counsel regarding the storm surrounding Lawrence Brazelton. He figured that the same accusations of collusion and corruption would be leveled and the administration would be accused of tampering with an ongoing investigation. That call had not come.

In Washington, silence was an alarm. Sounding loud, it warned of the calm before the storm. Chase had not heard from several key sources within the different departments regarding the progress of the investigation into the whereabouts of Lawrence. That fact, coupled with the lack of noise emanating from the Office of the Independent counsel, had Chase spooked. Silence was golden, but the silence from the Independent Counsel's office was eerie. Something was wrong. Chase began to question the sanity behind his brief involvement with the Group.

Paul Justin knew Lawrence was right. He knew he was not bluffing. Lawrence held all the cards so he phoned Andrews and talked with the pilot that would take Kelly and Lawrence to their unknown destination. He gave the pilot his instructions and hung the phone up. He looked at the door, half expecting to see the man from the clothing department. He realized that it was not that easy and that Lawrence wouldn't send him until he was on board the plane and on his way to wherever.

Kenneth Jeffreye waited along with Paul Justin. Each man grew more anxious by the minute. The one common bond the two men shared was a profound love for their country and the judicial system.

Anyone who threatened the country they loved and anyone who would tarnish that, which so many had worked and died for, would to be brought to justice, with no exceptions. In this particular instance, they were not dealing with every day common criminals, but with men who had for the most part taken an oath to watch over, guide, and protect this great nation. That was the source of their anxiety, the need to close the books on these unsavory traitors to the country they respected and loved.

Lawrence watched as the sleek leer jet circled the airfield once and then made its approach. As the planes wheels hit the ground, Lawrence began to feel the emotion build. The plane approached the end of the runway and stopped. Lawrence watched as the door opened. Kelly looked out before walking down the steps. Upon seeing him, she raced towards the car where he was waiting. He exited, and they embraced in a clutch that was reminiscent of a scene straight out of a movie. She grabbed the sides of his face and looked into his eyes. Both of them were now crying.

"Peanut, your ok," she said.

"I wasn't, but now I am," he replied.

They continued their embrace, parting occasionally to kiss. Lawrence motioned for her to go to the plane, and he would join her momentarily. He retrieved the cell phone from the front seat and dialed.

"Lucky, make the drop," he said.

"You got it boss. We gonna meet back at the yard or what? Lucky asked.

"No, we are done my friend. The man is going to give you a package. It is yours, you earned it, and I owe you at least that much," he said.

"But I was just beginning to have fun," Lucky replied.

"So long my friend," Lawrence said.

He tossed the phone into the front seat and took a moment to look around. He was in Falls Church for the last time. This is where it had all begun, and appropriately, this is where it was going to end. A tear ran down his cheek, as thoughts of his wife and son passed briefly. He looked towards the sky and winked in the direction of what he thought to be heaven. He had vindicated his life and the name his wife and son had been so proud of. He knew that they were happy. He had finally made all the wrongs right again.

Deep in his heart, at the core of his soul, he felt their joy for him and their encouragement for him to move on. They had accompanied him on this journey. They had given him strength and purpose. He knew that they would want him to be happy. He had worked so hard in his life, and he had lost so much. He deserved a fresh start, a new life, and an opportunity to know joy once again. With one last look, he turned and boarded the plane.

# EPILOGUE

Lawrence and Kelly flew to South America. They made several stops and changed modes of transportation several times before winding up in the Caribbean, Cozumel to be exact. From the quaint villa they purchased, located on the beach next to the crystal blue waters, they watched an empire crumble.

Lawrence has since begun practicing law on a limited basis. He does legal work for the less fortunate, people who otherwise could not afford it. It is his way of continuing to give thanks for his newfound happiness.

Preston A. Wesley became the first sitting President to be sent to prison. There were no deals and no pardons issued. Murder, corruption, and a blatant disregard of the law was one thing he could not spin into favor with the American public.

The other members of the Group faced similar fates. Lawrence never knew the names of the men in the Dogwatch, and for that matter, neither did anyone but Mike Baker. As a result, Conner and his men now sell their services to the highest bidder.

Ironically, the Vice President did not suffer in the eyes of the voting public and was elected as the first President of the next century. Chase Walters is now the Chief of Staff for the new President, and to this day, knowledge of his limited involvement with the Group remains a secret.

Paul Justin was appointed to the next open seat on the Supreme Court. The Independent Counsel statute was re-introduced and passed by an overwhelming majority. Lucky, well, he continues to be Lucky. With the money he received for his assistance, he went legit. Well, as close to legitimate as was possible for his character.

The scars were deep and the country had suffered. But this country and her people would bounce back. After all, the American dream stands for freedom, liberty, and the pursuit of happiness.

As Lawrence reflected on the events that had brought him to this point in time, he came to certain realizations. The turn of the century had passed. The vision conceived by the founders of this great nation in reference to the structure and nature of government has drifted farther and farther from its original course and ultimate destination.

Gone are the ideals that embodied political aspirations of generations past, whose sole purpose was to aspire to office, to step in and serve his fellow man, and bring with him the wisdom of a life's work. Those intrinsic values have been replaced with individuals that have earned the moniker "*Career Politicians.*"

We are in the process of reaping what we have sown, he thought.

### *The End*

# About The Author

A self proclaimed native of Arizona, E.L. Burton began his writing career late in life. Diagnosed with a degenerative eye disease and the prognosis of eventual blindness, he left the confines of corporate America to pursue his dream of becoming an author. His first novel, *$oft Money*, was inspired by the recent debates over the need for campaign finance reform. He is currently working on his second novel. That work is yet untitled, it centers on the recent random acts of violence and the debate over the need for additional gun control measures. E.L. Burton lives in Gilbert Arizona with his wife Kelly, and their dog Taffy.